# OBAMA UNMASKED

# OBAMA UNMASKED

## Did Slick Hollywood Handlers Create the Perfect Candidate?

## By Floyd Brown and Lee Troxler

**Merril Press**
**Bellevue, Washington**

*Obama Unmasked is published by*
Merril Press, P.O. Box 1682, Bellevue, WA 98009
www.merrilpress.com
Phone: 425-454-7008

*Distributed to the book trade by*
Midpoint Trade Books, 27 W. 20th Street,
New York, N.Y. 10011
www.midpointtradebooks.com
Phone: 212-727-0190


FIRST EDITION

Library of Congress Cataloging-in-Publication Data
Brown, Floyd, 1961-
  Obama unmasked : did slick Hollywood handlers create the perfect
candidate? / by Floyd Brown and Lee Troxler.
     p. cm.
  ISBN 978-0-936783-59-8
 1. Obama, Barack--Public opinion. 2. Obama, Barack--Ethics.
3. Obama, Barack--Political and social views. 4. Public relations
and politics--United States 5. Public opinion--United States 6.
Presidential candidates--United States--Biography. 7. Legislators-
-United States--Biography. 8. Presidents--United States--
Election--2008. 9. United States--Politics and government--2001- 10.
United States--Race relations--Political aspects. I. Troxler, Lee. II.
Title.
  E901.1.O23B76 2008
  328.73092--dc22

                                        2008030900

*Printed in the United States of America*

**Dedicated to the Memory of
Ronald Wilson Reagan**

# *Contents*

# II. Create the "Look" Democrats Crave, but...

# III. Will We End Up Living In An Obamanation?

Destroying what's left of quality healthcare.

Censoring conservatives on the radio.

Strangling business with sweeping regulations.

Hey all you in the Middle East, "Get along!"

Delivering $10 a gallon gas to a pump near you.

Appointing shifty radicals and Clinton retreads.

# *Introduction*

Late on the night of January 20, 2009, the next Commander-in-Chief will be driven from the inaugural podium, parade, and festivities to the Oval Office, where he will be met by a national security staff ready with the latest "threat briefing."

Will the lunatic Iranian President Mahmoud Ahmadinejad be moving nuclear missiles into Venezuela? Will Syria's Bashar al-Assad be ready to hammer Tel Aviv through Lebanese proxies? Has Venezuela's Hugo Chavez made gains in his scheme to shutdown U.S. oil supplies? And what of the other unhinged madmen—North Korea's Kim Jong-Il, Sudan's Hassan al-Bashir, Zimbabwe's Robert Mugabe, and of course Osama bin Laden?

All kinds of bad boys are hanging around the global water cooler these days. How would a President Obama respond to their threats?

By his own account, Obama would consider it a priority to meet at once with every evil thug out there—without precondition. A stroll down the Champs Elysees with Ahmadinejad would make for a great photo opp—two men of Muslim heritage, posing together in an emerging Muslim nation, one of them concealing a knife behind his back.

What could possibly have brought our nation to this point? How could we elevate a man by the name of Barack Hussein Obama to the most powerful position on earth?

It is a question we may all be asking as the chads settle late in the evening on November 4th, 2008. Or, if Obama fails in his historic quest, it may be because of new discoveries about the people who brought him into this world, who groomed him for this moment in time, and who now see themselves on the cusp of controlling a superpower—a lifelong dream of these people, these handlers.

This is their story—some of it is widely known, but other critical plot points appear for the first time in these pages, creating the full and complete story of Obama's remarkably swift rise to power.

It's a story told in three parts. First—the long search for a liberal hunk of clay fresh enough to be thrown on the potter's wheel of invented truth. Next—the mischievous work of many slippery and clay-muddied hands to shape a Presidential candidate Democrats could fall in love with. Lastly—a query into the kind of Obama-nation we could expect.

It's a story told in a hypermediated time, when collapsing news cycles, instant analyses, blogospheric rants, and YouTubed distortions of every political event give us fractured characters, twisted plot lines, and often unsatisfying endings.

It's a story told with the help and hindrance of a million other authors. For in this election, anyone with a computer can be a political animal, chewing on an endless supply of information, spitting the bones at any opinion they find disagreeable.

Our goal then has been to filter and organize this vast sea of information, add several of our own election-tipping discoveries, and leave you to your good judgment about Obama the possible President.

Along the way, we hope to lend perspective to many important questions that aren't likely to receive a satisfactory airing in this election cycle. Questions such as:

Why is Obama trying so hard to deny that he **was born and raised Muslim?**

What was Obama's father doing with **communist organizers** just days before the Cuban Missile Crisis? Moreover, what was the Father trying to imprint on the Son?

What did Obama mean when he described the **Muslim call to prayer** as *"one of the prettiest sounds on Earth at sunset"?*

Does Obama's conversion to Christianity make him an **apostate** "whose blood may be shed" by the devout nutcases in Islam?

In the 1850s, when Republicans were fighting for emancipation, were Obama's **ancestors shackling** the wrists of Negroes in Africa?

When Obama was a full-time slacker—doing drugs and drinking heavily, did it **stunt his development** in any way?

Has Obama changed since he spoke of the *"coldness of capitalism"* and told his communist mentor he felt like *"a spy behind enemy lines"*?

Did Obama use affirmative action to get into Harvard? On the occasions that Obama's **hidden side**—his imperious, mercurial, self-righteous nature—has erupted into public, what has been the outcome?

When Obama is labeled **Halfrican**, what is the point?

Michelle Obama doesn't **really hate** America, does she? When Mrs. Obama says she is obligated to put blacks before whites, is she **just pandering,** or is she speaking honestly? With the Obama's so often *not* on speaking terms, which of them would be sleeping on the couch in the White House?

How easily can Obama be bought? Unsealing the federal indictment against **his pal Tony "the Fixer" Rezko** should reveal plenty.

As an Illinois Senator, why did Obama vote "Present" a record-setting 130 times? When Obama did vote on important issues in Springfield, why did he vote the **Democratic Socialists of America** party line *every* time?

How was **"The Cult of Obama"** manufactured?

They say Obama has overcome **great oppression**. They are correct, but not in the way they think.

What "change" did Obama bring to the U.S. Senate when he had the chance?

Who is the only President who was **less prepared** for the job than Obama? Who has made more **gaffes** on the campaign trail—Barack Obama or Dan Quayle? Would Obama's **resume** be enough if he was white?

Is Obama's **patriotism** heartfelt, or merely convenient?

What does Obama's **secret addiction** reveal about his character?

What did Obama and George Soros agree to in their final meeting just before Obama announced his candidacy? Is George Soros really planning an **"October Surprise"** to make himself a fortune and Obama a President? The ingenious way George Soros fashioned Obama into **"a man of the people."** How many voters will approve of their Commander-in-Chief handing military policy over to MoveOn.org's unhinged fanatics?

He's JFK, he's MLK, why he's Mary Kay—Obama's **special place** in the hearts of the Leftstream Media.

Will Obama come clean and admit that it is **not racism** keeping his black brothers and sisters down? In short, will Obama be honest?

Why did Obama **actively seek** out Louis Farrakhan's blessing? Though he has "publicly" denounced his old friend Farrakhan, Obama still employs many **Farrakhan acolytes** in high-level positions—what does this signify? What have black leaders **demanded** in return for their support?

After 20 years of jumping up and down in the aisles to the gentle riffs of **"Kill whitey!"** sermons, can Obama just walk away?

Would a President Obama put his pastor in charge of incorporating **Ebonics** into the curriculum of our public schools?

Should we care that Rashid Khalidi is **obsessed** with an Obama victory?

How many of Obama's radical professor and unrepentant terrorist friends would **take senior posts** in an Obama Administration?

Did Obama seek the endorsement from the Arab musician known for the 2001 hit, **"Hey People, It Was Only a Tower"**?

In the end, is Obama any different from Al Sharpton or Jesse Jackson before him, or is he yet another **race-baiter**, only smoother?

Is the big wild card in this election, **Oprah?**

When Obama says he will pull troops out of Iraq, or not; when Obama says he will never use nuclear weapons, or not; when Obama says he will always talk to our enemies, or not; what are we to think, or not?

Why are so many **Islamofascists** both sworn to the destruction of America and actively campaigning for Obama?

What **special rights** could Muslims demand, and receive, with Obama in the Oval Office?

After refusing to condemn MoveOn.org for calling General Petraeus a **war criminal**, how could Obama be an effective Commander-in-Chief?

After Obama raises taxes the first time but doesn't get the revenue he needs, will he **raise taxes** a second time? And how high? Is the rumor true that a quick perusal of Obama's home library would find a *Complete Idiot's Guide to Taxes* on the shelf? How high would the average family's taxes increase under Obama?

Is it fair to conclude that Obama would put a gun to the head of an **unborn child**, but ban all other uses of that gun?

Is it true that Obama would create a **new federal agency**, the Department of Planned Parenthood?

One Obama says he will force states to allow same-sex marriages; the other Obama says states can make their own decisions; one of these two Obama's is *lying*.

The Supreme Court has now ruled definitely on the **Second Amendment**, but that can't stop Obama legislation which would force gun stores to move out into the empty deserts.

Why is Obama pushing the same 1930s trade policies that made the **Great Depression** so globally devastating?

What did Obama promise union bosses that caused them to commit **$1 Billion** to winning this election?

Will **ObamaCare** drive good doctors out of healthcare leaving us to the mercy of, well, of who?

Is Obama's promise to restore the Fairness Doctrine the guaranteed death knell of **conservative talk radio?**

5

Do businessmen truly understand the tangle of ***workplace regulations*** they'll see from Obama's labor watchdogs?

Will American Jews continue supporting Obama when his sympathy for the ***downtrodden Palestinians*** becomes official U.S. policy?

Why Obama's energy policies are guaranteed to deliver ***$10 gas*** before the end of his term.

Will Obama appoint shifty Chicago radicals or Clinton retreads to senior posts, or both?

And, in the final analysis, is it fair to conclude that Obama offers only the simple slogan of "change" because he has little else to offer?

Obama appears to be a fine man, handsome and intelligent. But of his plans for the Presidency … well, we know little. He has been thoroughly masked by his handlers in Hollywood, New York, and Washington. His very survival as a plausible candidate for the presidency now depends on his keeping the mask securely in place.

So, in these pages we peel back the mask to reveal the man, his true political leanings, and our expectations for an Obama-nation.

Few books are written in hopes of being unnecessary in just a few months—but this is one of those books. Our highest hope is that this book will be remaindered on November 5, 2008, because Obama has been told by voters that he's not ready for such an important job. Our deepest fear is that voters will say otherwise.

# I. Begin With A Good Hunk of Clay, but...

For a half-century since John Kennedy, the Democratic Party has searched for a leader with charisma and character—someone capable of inspiring a nation to the party's great ideals. Along the way, two things happened:

Those ideals went to seed, and Bill Clinton arrived with all the charisma, but none of the character, setting the party back further. But then along came the perfect hunk of clay—and the party's handlers could see an array of possibilities taking shape. They were very pleased, at first anyway.

In this first section, we look at the promise of Obama, and contrast it with reality.

# 1. Is Obama Even Half The Man He Claims To Be?

## Was Obama truthful about his "Muslim" upbringing?

Obama is often asked about his unique lineage, and he gladly volunteers:

> My father was from Kenya, and a lot of people in his village were Muslim. He didn't practice Islam. Truth is he wasn't very religious. He met my mother. My mother was a Christian from Kansas, and they married and then divorced. I was raised by my mother. So, I've always been a Christian.[1]

Always been a Christian – unequivocal words. The record shows that Obama's father, Barack Hussein Obama Sr. was, in fact, born on the shores of Lake Victoria in Alego, Kenya. He met Stanley Ann Dunham of Wichita, Kansas, in a Russian language class at the University of Hawaii. They fell in love, he just twenty-three and she just eighteen. Sometime in late 1960, the two slipped off to Maui and apparently married. There are no records that Obama's parents were ever legally married. But more important than whether Obama is a bastard, is the true identity of the father.

When Barack Sr. first came to America, before he met Barack Jr.'s mother, he'd left a pregnant wife and child back in Kenya. And later, when he returned to Africa, he took yet another American woman with him, eventually marrying her and having two additional children.

By most counts, the polygamist Barack Sr. fathered nine children by four wives. This much is widely known.

But we have uncovered details on the private meetings of Barack Sr. that have not been widely reported, not been shredded in the blogs, not mentioned in Barack Jr.'s book—but this discovery helps explain why Barack Jr. has spent a lifetime in search of a father who was an avowed communist.

On Mothers Day 1962, when Barack Jr. was just nine months old, his father slipped out the back door, as he often did. On this occasion he attended the "Hawaii Peace Rally" at Ala Moana Park. Also attending were 250 of the most controversial names of the time, including Bertrand Russell, Linus Pauling, Albert Schweitzer, and Philip Morrison. Each was a giant in his field, as well as a communist sympathizer or covert organizer. Also on hand were thirty-five members of Young Americans for Freedom (YAF), picketing the rally. One of these YAF members contacted San Francisco radio talk shot host Brian Sussman recently to recount the events of the time. He even dug up a dusty old YAF newsletter from 1962 to corroborate the story.

So what was Barack Sr. doing at the communist rally?

This was a dangerous time in U.S.-Soviet relations. Just six weeks earlier John Kennedy had met Nikita Khrushchev in Vienna, and been judged "weak" by the Soviet leader. Nuclear missiles were being moved into Cuba, and in three months the world would stand at the brink. Communists were infiltrating every institution they could in an attempt to undermine the U.S. from within.

These "peace rallies" were a front for those seeking to turn prominent Americans against their nation, in the hopes others would follow. Barack Sr. played a role in these treasonous activities. And within a year he would find the doors of Harvard opened for him. He would take off—leaving his family behind—never to return.

Before he walked out, however, he had left a fierce imprint on Barack Jr. By the boy's own account, much of his early years were spent in a vain search for the man and the ideal and fantasy that was his father. The search was so consuming that he authored a book about his many dreams of his father.  Why such a passion to know the father who deserted him?

Child psychologists have filled books on this subject, the gist of which is: the child spends a lifetime trying to impress, and win the love and approval of the absent father.  For Barack Jr. this means spending a lifetime trying to impress a man who had left Kenya, enrolled in the University of Hawaii to take Russian language classes, and had dedicated himself to the global communist struggle to overthrow America.

**This begins to explain many of the default political leanings of Barack Obama Jr. that we will see unfolding in this book.**

His claims about his mother, Stanley Ann Dunham are also dubious. He describes her as a Christian when the situation suits him. She was called Ann and her friends knew her to be a committed atheist and leftist.  In a moment of honesty, Obama said that his mother was in heaven despite her non belief. While speaking at a town hall forum in North Carolina on March 26, 2008, he said she was "not a believer." He continued, "But she was the kindest, most decent, generous person that I have ever known," Obama said. "I'm sure she is in heaven, even though she may not have subscribed to everything that I subscribe to."

When Obama was six years old, his mother married another Muslim man, an Indonesian oil manager, by the name of Lolo Soetoro.  The family followed Soetoro the Muslim back to Indonesia for the years 1967-71.  Obama first attended a Catholic school, Fransiskus Asisi, where he was officially enrolled as a Muslim.[2]

Several sources have stepped forward to confirm that at the time Obama was a Muslim, practicing Islam, and active in the Muslim community.

A blogger who goes by "An American Expat in Southeast Asia" has confirmed that, "Barack Hussein Obama was registered under the name 'Barry Soetoro' serial number 203 and entered the Franciscan Asisi Primary School on 1 January 1968 and sat in class 1B ... Barry's religion was listed as Islam."[3]

*Los Angeles Times* reporter Paul Watson has spoken with a number of Indonesians who knew Obama in Jakarta. All confirmed that Obama:

> Was registered by his family as a Muslim at both schools he attended [and that Obama] occasionally followed his stepfather to the mosque for Friday prayers.[4]

Obama's former school principal, Tine Hahiyary, says she recalls Obama studied the Quran in Arabic:

> At that time, I was not Barry's teacher, but he is still in my memory ... I remember that he studied 'mengaji [reciting the Quran][5]

His principal also noted that the *mengaji* was not intended for students desiring a secular education, but by those seeking more religious study.[6]

A reporter with the *Toronto Star*, Haroon Siddiqui, paid a visit to the Jakarta school Obama attended and found "*three of his teachers have said he was enrolled as a Muslim.*"

Other Indonesians tell the same story. His friend at the time, Zulfin Adi, says Obama "*was Muslim. He went to the mosque. I remember him wearing a sarong.*" Another friend, Rony Amir, describes Obama as "*previously quite religious in Islam.*"

Obama's half sister, Maya Soetoro-Ng, confirms that "*... my whole family was Muslim, and most of the people I knew were Muslim,*" and they attended the mosque "*for big communal events,*" but not every Friday.[7]

And finally, we are told by Obama himself in his memoirs that he would often get into trouble for making faces during Quranic studies.[8] So he was clearly attending Muslim religious classes. And according to Nicholas Kristof of *The New York Times*, Obama was such a good student he can still, after thirty-five years, recite the opening lines of the Muslim call to prayer "*with a first-rate accent.*"[9]

**Obama has described the Muslim call to prayer as "*one of the prettiest sounds on Earth at sunset.*"** This is how the call to prayer begins:

*Allah is Supreme! Allah is Supreme!*
*Allah is Supreme! Allah is Supreme!*
*I witness that there is no god but Allah*
*I witness that there is no god but Allah*
*I witness that Muhammad is his prophet...*

Yet Obama insists he has always been a Christian.

Even Obama's own half brother, Malik Obama, has confirmed that Obama is Muslim. In an interview with Israeli Radio, he wished his brother success on behalf of all the Obama's of Kenya. And he added that his brother "could be a good President for the Jewish people, despite his Muslim background."[10]

It's hard to get more independent confirmations of the truth than this. Yet Obama's campaign website[11] takes great offense at the whole idea that Obama has a Muslim background:

> *Barack Obama Is Not and Has Never Been a Muslim ...*
> *Obama never prayed in a mosque. He has never been*
> *a Muslim, was not raised a Muslim, and is a committed*
> *Christian.*

So what's going on here?

In Islam, religion passes from the father to the child. Barack Hussein Obama, Sr. named his boy Barack Hussein Obama, Jr. Of note, only Muslim children are named "Hussein." Obama writes in his memoir that his father was born into the Luo tribe in Nyangoma-Kogelo, Siaya District, Kenya. And his grandfather was a prominent and wealthy farmer who converted to Islam. Obama traces his male ancestral line in Africa back twelve generations.

But according to one source, *The U.S. Veteran Dispatch*, one little dark secret from his family's past has been conveniently buried:

> *In the 18th century, Muslim slavers moved into the*
> *interior of Kenya for the purpose of exploiting blood*
> *rivalries between local tribes. Muslims encouraged*
> *warring tribes, Obama Jr.'s Luo ancestors included, to*
> *capture "prisoners of war" and sell them into slavery.*[12]

**The Dispatch argues that Obama's African forebears not only owned slaves, they were active slave traders who would** capture their enemies, march them to the coast, and sell them to Arab slave traders who had contracts to fill in Europe and the Middle East.

The Luo tribe came to Kenya from Southern Sudan and Somalia and they were active slave traders. Journalist Kenneth Lamb has written:

> They operated under an extended grant from Queen Victoria, who gave them the right to continue the slave trade in exchange for helping the British defeat the Madhi Army in southern Sudan and the Upper Nile region. But telling America's black community that while their ancestors were breaking the shackles of slavery, Mr. Obama's ancestors were placing those shackles upon their wrists would hardly play as an Oprah Winfrey best-seller.[13]

Instead of getting answers, more questions are raised:

## Is Obama an American citizen eligible to run for President?

Obama says he was born at the Queen's Medical Center in Honolulu, Hawaii, on August 4, 1961. Despite much controversy about Obama's birth location, it seems that he was born in Hawaii, and he is eligible to become President of the United States, under Article Two of the Constitution.

Nevertheless, when journalists latched onto this issue of his birthplace based on internet allegations of a foreign birth, Obama's handlers went right to work producing a birth certificate and posting it conspicuously on Obama's own website. It looked like something Obama dug out of a shoebox in the attic— old, faded, very much real. It listed his name as Barack Hussein Obama. But following the "coincidence" of the birth records from Honolulu being "unavailable" for the day of August 4, 1961, then the sudden appearance of a birth certificate raises as many questions as it answers.

Then the whole "CitizenGate" matter turned weirder. The leading left-wing website Daily Kos (pronounced "chaos", if you want to know what makes liberals proud) posted a copy of Obama's birth certificate and began insisting *a bit too strenuously* that the certificate was genuine.

Eyebrows raised across the globe. Investigators went to work. Early in July 2008, an Israeli newspaper, *Israel Insider,* announced a startling discovery: A man named Jay McKinnon had implicated himself in the forgery of a Hawaii birth certificate similar to the one endorsed as genuine by the Barack Obama campaign. McKinnon is a document specialist trained by the Department of Homeland Security, but apparently not trained well enough, because next teams of forensics experts swooped in, and began ripping apart the Daily Kos birth certificate fiber by fiber. What they found was shocking! One board certified forensics expert, with thousands of investigations to his credit, put the Daily Kos certificate and an actual blank Hawaiian State certificate under a microscope and analyzed them.

> *The security borders do not match. Literally. They are not even close to identical ... looking closer at the [Daily Kos] certificate (magnified to 400%) clearly shows inconsistencies in the security border such as cut and paste marks and overlaying of the side borders where they meet the top and bottom.*

Other forensics experts weighed in, detailing even more inconsistencies in the "security patterns" and "hue values" in the Daily Kos certificate. One expert's conclusion:

> *I am convinced that the certificate is a fake (and not really a very good one) and I went into this with a completely open mind (something the Obamanationalists seem to have lost). I also have to say that everyone who has been looking into this federal crime (and it is a federal*

*crime even if the certificates were never meant to be used for identification) have done a stupendous job…*

If only Hawaiian state officials would comment on Obama's birth certificate issue, then the matter could be laid to rest. In the absence of official comment, we are left to wonder about Obama's citizenship. Shouldn't we be clear on this—before it becomes a genuine CitizenGate?

Especially in light of Obama's upbringing…

## Why does Obama insist he was never a Muslim?

With so many questions lingering, it was a natural for certain reporters to go looking for stones unturned. *Insight* magazine claimed in a January 2007 article that Obama spent at least four years in Indonesia attending a *madrassa*—a radical Islamic school known to teach terrorism. It was a gossipy article, with the "tip" apparently coming from Hillary's campaign. But the inference was that Obama's school was Wahabist and that he was being tutored in the radical, America-hating Wahabism that our country is fighting today.

Snopes.com, the fact-checking organization, was quick to call *Insight's* claim exceedingly far-fetched:

> *The large Indonesian community resident in Mecca was a medium through which knowledge about Wahabism reached Indonesia, but the community itself appears to have remained virtually immune to Wahabi influences. In reality there was little direct influence of Wahabism on Indonesian reformist thought until the 1970s.*[14]

Apparently the story was not true, and Insight should never have printed it without a little fact-checking first. But with the story out, Obama swung into damage control mode because the story raised a tangential question in the minds of voters—a very important tangential question:

Is this man trying to hide something from us, something very damaging?

We most definitely want to know who the man is, what he stands for, and how he intends to lead. If he's afraid to tell us who he is—afraid, frankly, to admit to beginning life as a Muslim, then he's not being straight up with us.

Having been born and raised a Muslim and then converting to Christianity makes him neither more nor less qualified to be President. But if he has been actively hiding important facts about his upbringing, as appears to be the case, this points to a deceit, which carries with it profound implications about his suitability to be President. If he will lie about his religion, what else won't he tell Americans if he actually is elected and takes control of our military and our security?

At one point in his campaign, Obama saw the corner he had backed himself into, and he began a tortured process of baby-step retractions.

Two months after Obama had insisted that he was "never" a Muslim, Obama's campaign issued this nuanced note:

*Obama has never been a practicing Muslim.*[15]

And by adding the word *"practicing"* Obama climbed onto the slippery slope of modern politics, calling into question the truthfulness of everything he says, inviting comparisons to Hillary's and Bill's finely crafted lies, causing people to wonder if Obama is truly the fresh voice of "new politics" he claims to be.

So what is the takeaway from all this?

Put yourself in Obama's shoes. You're bright. You're going places. The whole black thing is working for you. The last thing you want to be straddled with is Muslim Heritage. So what do you do? You tell little white lies. You justify, you rationalize, you bargain with your ego. You learn to tap dance with the ethics you profess to hold sacred. And all is well until you run for President, and people want to know who you really are. For them, all of the fuzzy fabrications are uncomfortably familiar … they've seen the tap dancers before.

> *It depends on what the meaning of 'is' … I can't find my law firm billing records … I voted for the war before I voted against it … I was never a practicing Muslim.*

## Was Obama even truthful about his parents?

It is not uncommon for a young man of substance to gild the accomplishments of his youth, or to invent genealogies that paint his family in a more sympathetic light. To add some scrapes and scratches, dents and bruises to the slick exterior of manicured lawns and healthy bank accounts really isn't lying ... it's just adjusting the truth, right? After all, isn't a rags-to-riches story much more fun than a riches-to-riches story?

So we don't get too exercised when Obama tells rapt audiences that *"my father ... grew up herding goats"* when Kenyan records clearly show that Obama's grandfather, Hussein Onyango Obama was a wealthy farmer, and Obama's father was a child of privilege, not privation.[16] His father was a distinguished scholar, not a goat herder.

We fondly hope that whatever biographical flourishes Obama felt compelled to invent as a young adult, will no longer be required now that he's a bit older.

## The larger, more important question of "death threats."

Late in the primary campaign, as Hillary grew increasingly afraid her historic female candidacy would be derailed by an upstart nobody, she threw the kitchen sink at Obama.

Her private investigators had been working hard, and their first "leak" to the press had been the *"attended a madrassa"* story. Then came the offhand "observation" that Obama couldn't survive 100 days in office without being gunned down by a mad assassin.

It was a low moment, even by Clintonian standards. That Martin Luther King Jr., Malcolm X, John Kennedy, and Robert Kennedy had all been gunned down in the 1960s in large or full part because of their advancement of civil rights for blacks, was immaterial to Hillary's observations. Hillary knew it. If Obama is elected, we have every confidence that our United States Secret

Service will raise the bar on Presidential protection and keep our President safe from deranged assassins.

But what of deranged Muslims, or even sane ones? That's the story Hillary did not let slip, and it could be an even more important story. In a series of investigative articles, Robert Spencer and Daniel Pipes have shown how **Obama's conversion from Muslim to Christian mark him as a *murtadd* or "someone whose blood may be shed."**[17] The religion of peace has strict rules about *murtadd*, which translates into "apostate" or someone who has forsaken Muhammad, the prophet of Islam. Pipes asks a critical question:

> *Although this is frequently denied ... his statement 'Whoever changes his religion, kill him' appears in numerous authoritative Islamic sources. So is Barack Obama under a death sentence?*

In Muslim eyes, being born to a Muslim male makes him a Muslim. All Muslims understand the full name of Barack Hussein Obama, to signify he was born Muslim. Obama's conversion to Christianity, in short, makes him a murtadd. In fact, this is the worst of all crimes in Muslim law—worse than murder, which the family of the victim may forgive.[18]

How might mainstream Muslims respond to an Obama charged with religious flip-flopping? Pipes asks:

> *Would they be angry at what they would consider his apostasy? That reaction is a real possibility, one that could undermine his initiatives toward the Muslim world.*

Obama's decision to leave Islam could complicate moderate Muslim nations' ability to cooperate in the war on Islamofascist terror.

How could Obama, for instance, call on the leaders of Islam to cease their approval of using little children as human bombs in crowded marketplaces?

In the eyes of Muslims, has he forsaken his spiritual heritage?

Has Obama abandoned his Muslim faith just as Judas turned away from Christianity?

Are the coins of the presidency more precious to Obama than the articles of his boyhood faith?

These are the kinds of questions devout Muslims may be asking. And these questions could compromise any attempt to press for human rights and democracy in Muslim nations. It could, in short, seriously cripple an Obama presidency.

Most likely, if the question of apostasy does take center stage, we will see a series of clean-shaven Islamic spokesmen appearing before the cameras, smiling in that condescending way that superior beings do, insisting that Islam teaches no such thing. Joining in will be the Leftstream Media, adding that anyone who utters apostasy and Obama in the same sentence is a clearly a racist bigot.

Together in common cause, the Islamic spokesmen and the Leftstream Media will use every opportunity to portray Obama as someone who is uniquely qualified to understand the Islamic world—and isn't that wonderful?

Yes, it would be wonderful unless a President Obama uses his unique understanding of the Islamic world to chart a course of appeasement and capitulation. More on his foreign policy agenda will be covered in Chapter 12.

## Another aimless child from another single-parent home.

Growing up in Indonesia in the 1960s was no bowl of cherries. The nation was torn by violent rebellion—the dictator Sukarno was overthrown and Communists were being massacred. Obama's second father was deeply scarred by these events, and he grew distant from Obama. His mother took a job as an embassy secretary to help pay for extra schooling for her son. She would, as Obama tells it, wake him at four in the morning to give him English lessons before formal school. Obama writes of his mother's belief in education:

*... a lonely witness for secular humanism, a soldier for New Deal, Peace Corps, position-paper liberalism. She would come home with books on the civil rights movement, the recordings of Mahalia Jackson, the speeches of Dr. King... Every black man was Thurgood Marshall or Sidney Poitier; every black woman Fannie Lou Hamer or Lena Horne. To be black was to be the beneficiary of a great inheritance, a special destiny, glorious burdens that only we were strong enough to bear.*

Obama could feel a fount of black pride growing inside of him, thanks to these teachings. But with events spiraling out of control in Indonesia, his mother sent him back to Hawaii to live with his grandparents. He was enrolled at Punahou, an elite prep school where white girls who had never seen a black boy wanted to touch his hair, and where white boys challenged him about his father—a member of the Luo tribe with a long history of cannibalism, brutal massacres of opposition tribes, and slave trading.

Obama wanted none of this attention, and dedicated himself instead to the carefree Hawaiian lifestyle—playing basketball, bodysurfing, goofing off. Obama recalls rather honestly:

*Some of the problems of adolescent rebellion and hormones were compounded by the fact that I didn't have a father. So what I fell into were these exaggerated stereotypes of black male behavior—not focusing on my books, finding respectability, playing a lot of sports.*[19]

Obama grew a big Afro hairdo and donned a stylish white open-collared leisure suit with fat lapels, trying to look urban black cool. Reportedly quite the dandy, he spent hours picking at his Afro to get it just right. His sister Maya recalls mussing his hair and being yelled at, *"Hey, don't touch the 'fro!"*

**By his senior year of prep school, Obama was a full-time slacker, doing drugs and drinking heavily.** Somehow, despite his mediocre grades and bum attitude, he managed to shine the admissions officers of Occidental College in Southern California.

How he wangled entrance to yet another expensive private school with little known family money remains a mystery. But by his own account, Obama began coming into his own at Occidental.

It wasn't long before he fell in with the rad-chic crowd, hanging at coffee houses with Marxist professors, feminist activists, and punk-rock poets all agitating for rebellion against "Whitey":

> When we ground out our cigarettes in the hallway carpet or set our stereos so loud that the walls began to shake, we were resisting bourgeois society's stifling constraints...

Obama thought he was writing of rebellion. Others thought Obama was confusing rebellion with partying and getting high.[20] During one of those late-night rages, a coed asked why he went by the name "Barry" when his given name was Barack. He explained that Barack meant "blessed" in Arabic, and that his father's side was Muslim, but he preferred Barry.

*"Do you mind if I call you Barack?"* she asked.

Click! Three decades later you can still hear the echoes of the light bulb that went off in Obama's head. "This 'Barack' thing might just get me farther down the road than 'Barry' ever will. Buh-Bye, Barry."

At Occidental, Obama steeped himself in the prominent black writers—W.E.B. Du Bois, James Baldwin, Langston Hughes, and Ralph Ellison—but by his own account, he was most stirred by Malcolm X, the father of black power and the leader of the Nation of Islam. This made sense, given the racial struggles of the time, and Obama's growing sense of "blackness."

Obama remembers a girl on campus who, like him, had come from a multi-racial background. He found her in tears one day because black people were trying to make her choose between black and white. It was black people, Obama conceded, who always made everything about race. He saw that white people could learn and evolve beyond their prejudices to become non-racial and non-judgmental, but black people were mired in the ancient mud of racism and seemed incapable of rising above it.

*"Only white culture had individuals,"* he wrote, not black culture.

This realization tore at Obama. One imagines that he didn't want to choose, perceiving himself as having left the mud and his make-believe world of goat-herding behind. But he was still searching for an identity—Barry desperately seeking Barack—, and it was most important to him to not be seen as "a sellout." So he chose his friends for the blackness of their skin and the leftness of their politics. But it wasn't enough. Unsatisfied with the radical-lite atmosphere of Occidental, Obama arranged to transfer to a hotbed of radical liberalism, Columbia University.

There in New York, in the center of the burgeoning "black power" movement, Obama attended communist rallies with Stokely Carmichael; he soaked in Jesse Jackson's rhyming vitriol, and marched when Jesse said march; he joined Ralph Nader's camp for a while as a shill for recycling; he reveled in the coke-addled, hedonist bazaar that was Harlem in the early 1980s; and yes, he probably attended a few classes at Columbia—little if anything is written about this stage in his life. He skips it almost entirely in his own memoirs. But he does speak of graduating and taking his first real job at Business International Corporation. The company offered consulting services to American companies operating overseas. And for a year, Obama produced how-to manuals on international business.

**He told his biographer, David Mendell that he loathed the job and was offput by the *"coldness of capitalism."***

**To his Communist Party mentor, Frank Marshall Davis, Obama confessed that he felt like *"a spy behind enemy lines."*[21]**

And in his memoirs, Obama elaborated on his growing sense of *"working class solidarity,"* identifying *"the real enemy"* as *"investment bankers ... politicians,"* and *"fat-cat lobbyists."* [22]

Young Obama appeared to be headed down the very path of European socialism that mainstream America was happily, and resolutely, consigning to the dustbin of history.

## Organizing the nation's largest group of blacks.

As Obama began to yearn for a life in politics, it was natural that he would gravitate to union organizing—the most liberal avenue he could have chosen. In his response to an advertisement to work on Chicago's South Side, known as the capital of the black community in America, there was no mistaking his intentions. As he wrote in his memoirs:

> *"Change won't come from the top... Change will come from a mobilized grass roots. That's what I'll do. I'll organize black folks. At the grass roots. For change."* [23]

He arrived in Chicago in June 1985 to work with the Developing Communities Project, which paid $13,000 a year. One didn't take such jobs for the money. He was tossed right away into the Roseland and Altgeld Gardens areas—where crushing poverty, raging violence, a cornucopia of drugs and homicidal crime were endemic, and where he was totally expected to fail. Still, he threw himself into this thankless job, focusing on the few small problems he could solve, taking baby steps with the hopeless and illiterate who had been told by successive generations of liberal politicians that their only job was to show up at the welfare office once a month.

Obama's guides at this point schooled him in the Alinsky method, named for the radical socialist Saul Alinsky who believed in agitating people so intensely, **making them so angry about their rotten lives that they "rub raw the sores of discontent" and take action to change** their lives. Alinsky's book, a bestseller in all the lefty bookshops, was titled *Rules for Radicals* and it was the lodestar for Obama's approach to politics on the street.

And yet, despite his earnestness and high energy, even Obama grew quickly disillusioned with organizing, and he wondered what might be in store for him next. When he sought guidance from one of his socialist mentors, he was advised to find himself a church.

## Searching for his "black future" in church.

Joining a black church was a smart way for a young man on the move in Chicago to address some gaps in his résumé *and* holes in his soul.

In his writings, however, Obama has repeatedly insisted that he was drawn to Trinity United and its Reverend Jeremiah Wright not so much for its career-boosting potential, but more to address the deeper longing in his soul. It's probably just coincidence that he chose a church widely considered among Chicago blacks to be the church of elites, attracting such celebrities as Oprah Winfrey.

Before Obama joined Trinity United, Reverend Wright warned him that the church was quite radical. Obama joined anyway, possibly because he was actively seeking to be blacker, and more like local voters. His half-Kenyan, half-Kansan skin swirled closer to caramel, while his Chicago pew-mates were more ebony toned. Obama wanted some kind of coherent identity in his African heritage. W.E.B. Du Bois has written in *Souls of Black Folk* of how:

> *[The black American] ever feels his two-ness—an American, a Negro; two souls, two thoughts, two unreconciled strivings; two warring ideals in one dark body, whose dogged strength alone keeps it from being torn asunder.*

And so Obama struggled to transcend the "two-ness", growing adept at slipping back and forth between black and white worlds, frightened by the realization that he belonged to neither. And in this passage into adulthood, no one supplied his need for racial identity as potently as Reverend Wright. In Wright's church, Obama found the racial community he hungered for.

Obama did not, by his own account, find any deep religious salve at Trinity. Instead, he remained tethered to his mother's religious views:

*For my mother, organized religion too often dressed up closed-mindedness in the garb of piety, cruelty and oppression in the cloak of righteousness. This isn't to say that she provided me with no religious instruction... the Bible, the Koran, and the Bhagavad Gita sat on the shelf alongside books of Greek and Norse and African mythology. On Easter or Christmas Day my mother might drag me to church, just as she dragged me to the Buddhist temple, the Chinese New Year celebration, the Shinto shrine, and ancient Hawaiian burial sites. But I was made to understand that such religious samplings required no sustained commitment on my part...*[24]

Obama's lack of attentiveness to the actual teachings of Trinity United would come back to bite him in twenty years. But for that moment in time, Obama had found a home.

# 2. Is Obama The First Product Of "Affirmative Action"?

In his memoirs, Obama is strangely silent about the decisions and events leading up to his acceptance at the Harvard Law School. He does not discuss, for instance, whether he was accepted on an affirmative action set-aside. One would think that a proud black man would trumpet such an occurrence as "proof" that affirmative action policies were yielding benefits. Didn't happen.

Barack doesn't toot the horn of affirmative action. Why? Could it be that he doesn't want to draw attention to his own affirmative action experience?

Harvard will neither confirm nor deny that Obama was admitted to their prestigious law school because of affirmative action. But it is safe to assume that Obama did apply for an African-American set aside. With his unimpressive academic career, it is unlikely he would have been admitted to Harvard otherwise.

## Fighting about "how best" to hate white America.

Harvard in the 1980s was locked in bitter ideological warfare. Liberals and conservatives waged battle on the big issues of the day, engaged on the foggy front of proper nouns in order to define themselves to themselves and the outside world. In the offices of the prestigious Law Review, black students couldn't agree how to refer to each other, or how the world should refer to them. Were they Blacks, African-Americans, American-Africans, Americans of African descent? This latter suggestion was discarded post haste—it was considered too forgiving of Whitey (though obviously the most descriptive, and technically correct). Inevitably the discussion became quite heated. As the columnist Clarence Page would later write:

*Race intrudes rudely on the individual's attempts to define his or her own identity. I used to be 'colored.' Then I was 'Negro.' Then I became 'black.' Then I became 'African American.' Today I am a 'person of color.' In three decades I have been transformed from a 'colored person' to a 'person of color.*[25]

Eager to quell the furor this issue was causing among his racially confused comrades, Obama stepped in with leadership:

*Whether we're called Black or African American doesn't make a whole heck of a lot of difference to the lives of people who are working hard, you know, living day to day, in Chicago, in New York. That's not what's going to make a difference in their lives...*[26]

Confirming this account of Obama's cool prevailing head was Brad Berenson, a classmate of Obama's who later served in Bush Justice Department. Berenson recalls:

*Barack always floated a little bit above those controversies and divisions. Barack made no bones about the fact that he was a liberal but you didn't get the sense that he was a partisan—that he allied himself with some ideological faction on the Review...*[27]

This flattering recollection of Obama notwithstanding, it's a shame that someone of Obama's rhetorical talents could not convince his black brothers to accept the fact that they were Americans; that white Americans had advanced the cause of equal rights at a pace unmatched anywhere on the globe; that they should be enormously appreciative of the advances made and now join in the constant task of making America an ever better place.

That's what a genuine "unifier" would have done.

Instead, Obama and his comrades at Harvard Law lent an intellectual boost to the Black Power movement, taking it from the streets to the classrooms, courtrooms, and community centers of America. And instead of presenting himself as an American running for President, Obama became the African-American running for President. In that case, shouldn't he and his media machine at least refer to his opponent as a Panamanian-Scot-English-American because Senator McCain was born at a Naval station in Panama to Scottish and English parents? While he's at it, shouldn't Obama come clean about the whole Harvard Law School experience?

Obama delights in telling audiences that he was the first "African-American" President of the Harvard Law Review. That is true, but *only* because they changed the job title from "Editor" to "President" just for him. Another "African-American," Charles Hamilton Houston, was Editor of the Review in 1919.[28] A small point, given Obama's academic accomplishments. But a small point that goes to veracity, something apparently in short supply at Harvard Law.

When Forrest Gump talked about his "box of chocolates," he could have been talking about Obama's box of truths, "You never know what you're gonna get."

## Racial pain—maybe, economic pain—no.

Obama's time at Harvard ushered the aspiring young leader further along a "sheltered' path—far removed from the working men and women he would later seek to represent.

He had spent his entire life in elite schools. His life experiences had not once overlapped with the day-to-day struggles that working Americans experience. He had not felt the genuine pain of not being able to provide for his family. He had, in his short stint as a community organizer, been given a grim tutorial in failed liberalism—that is true. There on the streets he had seen terrible poverty, and he had seen how the expectation of a welfare check made the streets even meaner. But he had grown into a young man without feeling what half of this country's working men and women experience every day. In the end, he had a nice house to go home to, tailored suits to wear, and good food to eat. He wanted for nothing.

His understanding of the American middle-class experience appears to have come from his Marxist textbooks. So he donned the mask of a "reformer" in the belief that this is what Middle America and South Chicago desired. He wore the mask, as well, to hide the essential part of him—the part he could not let anyone see. In the words of his biographer David Mendell:

> **What the public has yet to see clearly is his hidden side: his imperious, mercurial, self-righteous and sometimes prickly nature,** each quality exacerbated by the enormous career pressures that he has inflicted upon himself. He can be cold and short with reporters who he believes have given him unfair coverage. He is an extraordinarily ambitious, competitive man with persuasive charm and a career reach that seems to have no bounds. He is, in fact, a man of raw ambition so powerful that even he is still coming to terms with its full force. This drive is rooted in an effort to atone for his absent father's tragic failures, both as a Kenyan politician and as a family man...[29]

Overcoming his racially confused and deficient past seems to drive Obama with a ferocity that few of us feel. Mulattos often have their identities questioned, and that can be difficult to endure. It can make the child feel *inauthentic*—that is, neither black nor white. That *inauthenticity* can and often is generalized beyond race to character.

**When Obama is labeled *"Halfrican"* as he was by radio show host Brian Sussman in 2007, the point is *not* that Obama is of mixed-race.** The point is about his authenticity. Is he black, or really white, or what group does he identify with? Without a clear answer from Obama himself, people are left guessing.

Another man of mixed race, Shelby Steele, has written eloquently on Obama's quest for the presidency in a book titled, *A Bound Man*. It should be read by everyone interested in Obama's candidacy. Shelby speaks of the dilemma Obama faces in trying to wear a mask that appeals to black audiences without offending white audiences:

> *There is a price to be paid even for fellow-traveling with a racial identity as politicized and demanding as today's black identity. This identity wants to take over a greater proportion of the self than other racial identities do. It wants to have its collective truth—its defining ideas of grievance and protest—become personal truth. And then it wants to make loyalty to this truth a reflex within the self, within one's own thoughts, so that all competing thoughts are conceived in disloyalty. A perfectly internalized censorship. To be "authentically black" is to think more as a black than as one's self.*

And Shelby concludes:

**Does this disqualify Obama for the presidency? It may.**[30]

Even before Obama left New York for the streets of Chicago, he would be tested on his core beliefs on race. After Columbia, he fell in love with a white woman. They lived together for a year in their own cocoon of happiness. Then one day, while visiting her parents at the family's country house, Obama had something of an epiphany. His world and hers were too different ... too separate ... too incompatible. It wasn't that he wasn't accepted; *her* parents were gracious, and entirely welcoming. But *he* didn't belong.

Not long after, he met a woman named Michelle Robinson.

# 3. Does Michelle Obama Really Hate America?

When Michelle Robinson first met the new associate assigned to her supervision at her law firm Sidley Austin, a fellow named Barack Obama, she was hardly impressed. But then, she had a history of being less than impressed.

Back in her Princeton days, Michelle had produced a senior thesis titled "Princeton-Educated Blacks and the Black Community" in which she wrote:

> No matter how liberal and open-minded some of my White professors and classmates try to be toward me, I sometimes feel like a visitor on campus, as if I really don't belong.[31]

If this was all Michelle had written, Princeton would have not slapped a restriction on the distribution of her thesis—refusing media requests to view it until November 5, 2008. But Princeton and the Obama's were thwarted by enterprising bloggers who uncovered a copy of the full manuscript. It offers all kinds of insights into the potential future First Lady.

## Michelle's militant racism in black and white print.

In her thesis, Michelle laid out her displeasure with America going right back to the start, detailing how the nation was founded on *"crime and hatred."* Perhaps she would find more pleasure in the African experience where tribal elders sold young men to Arab slave traders to transport to the dozens of countries around the world where slavery existed?

Moving her analysis forward 200 years to race relations in the 1980s, Michelle argued that blacks should choose between being a *"separationist"* or an *"integrationist."* As for herself, Michelle put herself firmly in the separationist camp:

> *By actually working with the Black lower class or within their communities as a result of their ideologies, a separationist may better understand the desperation of their situation and feel more hopeless about a resolution as opposed to an integrationist who is ignorant to their plight.*

To this way of thinking, she would have her future husband, as part of his organizing efforts in South Chicago, tell the brothers to stay out of the system, find your own way, snub Whitey. Not only did she believe there had to be separate black and white societies in this country, but she made clear which of those societies she was siding with:

> **There was no doubt in my mind that as a member of the black community, I am obligated to this community and will utilize all of my present and future resources to benefit the black community first and foremost.**

So here are two follow-up questions for you, Michelle:

1. How as First Lady would you use the considerable resources of the White House to elevate blacks over whites in America?

2. Would you press your husband for anti-white affirmative action policies in the areas that have most grieved you?

Most disturbing was the conclusion of Michelle's thesis. She had sent out a questionnaire to 400 black alumni, seeking the benefit of their wisdom. Only 89 of 400 replied, and even that small sample did not share her views on distancing from Whitey. She was demonstrably agitated that the black alumni wished to "fit in" to America:

*I hoped that these findings would help me conclude that despite the high degree of identification with whites as a result of the educational and occupational path that black Princeton alumni follow, the alumni would still maintain a certain level of identification with the black community. However, these findings do not support this possibility.*

Michelle's thesis offers a clear view into the thinking of the person who would be closest to the President. It shows a woman whose bitterness is no small matter. As Michael Reagan reminds us:

*After being subjected to 8 years of the collegial presidency of Bill and Hillary, when we were told that when we got Bill we got Hillary as a bonus, it looks as if we are facing another twofer: Barack and Michelle. And the other half of the twofer is very different, she is down there in the trenches acting like the flame-throwing liberal activist she is. To know her, is to know what her husband really believes. [32]*

## Another President sleeping on the couch?

With the Clinton's gone, we could all be forgiven for exhaling at last and hoping that bedroom behavior of the First Couple would not be leading the evening newscast. But no, we have Michelle herself dissing her husband in public:

*What I notice about men, all men, is that their order is me, my family, God is in there somewhere, but 'me' is first. And for women, 'me' is fourth, and that's not healthy. [33]*

A good many women, and men, would disagree with Michelle's assessment of the sorry state of men. As for what her husband Barack thinks of Michelle's assessment, we know only what he wrote in his own autobiography. He spoke of the many times Michelle and he were *"not on speaking terms"* because of the pressures of his job. We don't pretend to be marriage counselors, but here are two tips for Michelle:

1. If you want to know what a real pressure cooker of a job is, review the photos of former Presidents and see how their hair turned gray in just a few short years. The before and after pictures will be especially instructive.

2. And please, should your husband win, give him the bed and you take the couch—we may need him to be alert.

## Michelle's speeches tell us if she's still bitter.

In fairness, Michelle, like her husband, was clearly searching for her own sense of identity in college, and her thesis alone should not be used to judge her. We can gain a fuller understanding of the ideals and beliefs that animate the current lady by examining her more current speeches.

Not too current, though. After the first several speeches Michelle gave on the campaign trail, the Obama handlers hauled her out to the woodshed for a good dressing down, and lessons in civility. Apparently, that's a difficult thing for her to master, as evidenced by her now most famous speech in Milwaukee:

> ***"For the first time in my adult life, I am proud of my country*** *because it feels like hope is making a comeback."*[34]

So once her husband became the frontrunner in the race, she became proud of America. As for the intelligence of her husband, Michelle says:

> *[Barack] is one of the smartest people you will ever encounter who will deign to enter this messy thing called politics.*[35]

How fortunate for us that he's willing to grovel in politics for our benefit. But still, both of these comments could be dismissed as the excitable utterances of a woman who is both proud of her husband and unaccustomed to the intense glare of the national stage. No such powder can cover over the troubling view of government evidenced in this speech at a Los Angeles rally.

> *[Barack] will require you to work ... he is going to demand that you shed your cynicism ... that you come out of your isolation, that you move out of your comfort zones. That you push yourselves to be better. And that you engage. Barack will never allow you to go back to your lives as usual, uninvolved, uninformed.*[36]

So the President's role is to tell us how to live our private lives. Is that the suggestion? Really? It would appear so from Obama's later reproach in Oregon:

> *We can't drive our SUVs and eat as much as we want and keep our homes on 72 degrees at all times ... and then just expect that other countries are going to say OK. That's not leadership. That's not going to happen.*[37]

So an Obama Administration would be telling us what kinds of cars we're allowed to drive, and how high we can turn the thermostat? And if our pals in France and Bolivia don't approve of the lifestyles we're living, then heads are going to roll?

Apparently, to hear Michelle tell it, our nation has lost its compass and we must rely on other countries to guide us—with Obama's help, of course:

> *We have to compromise and sacrifice for one another in order to get things done. That is why I am here, because Barack Obama is the only person in this who understands that. That before we can work on the problems, we have to fix our souls. Our souls are broken in this nation.*

How fortunate that Obama is here to help mend our broken souls, whether we like it or not! Another Michelle, the journalist Michelle Malkin, has summed up the candidate's wife's appeal, or lack thereof:

> *[Michelle] has been likened to John Kennedy's wife, what with her chic suits and pearls and perfectly coiffed helmet hair. But when she opens her mouth, Michelle Obama is less Jackie Obama and more Wendy W—as in Wendy Whiner, the constantly kvetching 'Saturday Night Live' character from the early 1980s...*[38]

Indeed Michelle's griping could become a *current* Saturday Night Live sketch, with Michelle griping about having to pay back her college loans. As Burt Prelutsky quipped:

> *Seven years at Ivy League schools and this woman still doesn't know how to spell gratitude.*[39]

A guilt-stricken white society smoothed her way through Princeton and Harvard Law, which led to her landing a high-paying job, and she's griping about her student loans.

No speech reveals more about the inner Michelle than the one she delivered in North Carolina just before that state's primary vote. **This is the kind of speech you would expect from Hugo Chavez, or Che Guevara, but not by a potential First Lady in 2008 America.** This speech is so revealing, we have excerpted several large portions:

> *... they set the bar. They say look, if you do these things, you can get to this bar, right? And then you work and you struggle, you do everything that they say, and you think you're getting close to the bar and you're working hard, and you're sacrificing, and then you get to the bar, you're right there, you're reaching out for the bar, you think you have it, and then what happens? They move the bar. They raise it up. They shift it to the left and to*

*the right. It's always just quite out of reach. And that's a little bit of what Barack has been experiencing. The bar is constantly changing for this man. Raise the money? Not enough. Build an organization? Not enough. Win a whole bunch of states? Not the right states. You got to win certain states. So the bar has been shifting and moving in this race, but the irony is, the sad irony is that that's exactly what's happening to most Americans in this country...*

*... what happens in that nation is that people do become isolated. They do live in a level of division, because see, when you're that busy struggling all the time, which most people that you know and I know are, that you don't have time to get to know your neighbor...*

*... and when you live in a nation with a vast majority of Americans are struggling to reach an ever-shifting and moving bar, then naturally, people become cynical. They don't believe that politics can do anything for them. So they fold their arms in disgust, and they say you know, I can't be bothered voting, because it has never done anything for me before. So let me stay home, let me not bother...*

*... then what happens in that kind of nation is that people are afraid, because when your world's not right, no matter how hard you work, then you become afraid of everyone and everything...*

*Fear is the worst enemy. It cuts us off from one another and our own families, and our communities, and it has certainly cut us off from the rest of the world. It's like fear creates this veil of impossibility, and it is hanging over all of our heads, and we spend more time now in this nation talking about what we can't do…*

*… our fear is helping us to raise a nation of young doubters, young people who are insular and they're timid. And they don't try, because they already heard us tell them why they can't succeed…*

This speaker is *not* running for President. But she is clearly an integral part of her husband's campaign. Her views will influence Obama's views if he becomes President. And her views are not ones that most Americans share.

## If Michelle campaigns for Obama, she must be scrutinized.

Campaigning in Tennessee, Obama had some advice for reporters about the care and handling of his wife:

*If they think that they're going to try to make Michelle an issue in this campaign, they should be careful because that I find unacceptable. The notion that you start attacking my wife, or my family … is just low class … Lay off my wife, all right?[40]*

Is this the kind of old-fashioned chivalry we admire in a man? Sure. But does Obama really think Michelle can campaign on his behalf and not be questioned? She can fire the arrows; but no return fire shall be allowed? That's not chivalry, that's childish.

Does Obama believe Michelle deserves "a pass" because she's a black woman? We don't think so—ours is color- and gender-blind nation. But if Michelle is going to campaign for Barack, then she is going to be asked the hard questions. Such as:

*Mrs. Obama, what do you mean when you call Obama "the fact guy" who 'seems to have a fact about everything. He can argue and debate about anything. It doesn't matter if he agrees with you, he can still argue with you. Sometimes, he's even right.*[41]

We'd like to know if Michelle was having a little harmless fun at her husband's expense, or if his argumentative spirit is hard on her and divorce may be in the picture, upsetting his ability to govern?

Michelle doesn't get a pass. If she wants to share recipes or her kid's grades, that's different. Her family's private life is off-limits—unless or until she shares it with us. But when she is speaking on behalf of her husband's campaign for the presidency, she had better expect to be accountable.

# 4. Is Obama Deeply Involved In Chicago Political Sleaze?

## Learning to play Chicago machine politics.

Fresh out of Harvard Law, Obama threw himself into New York politics for a spell, but soon he was back in his new adopted home, Chicago. Seeing once again the streets he had worked as a community organizer, Obama was struck by the depth of poverty and hopelessness. He wrote of his encounters:

> *Signs of decay accelerated throughout the South Side— the neighborhoods shabbier, the children edgier and less restrained, more middle-class families heading out to the suburbs, the jails bursting with glowering youth, my brothers without prospects.*[42]

Obama was clearly depressed by what he saw, and yearned to be able to help his brothers. But **absent from his writings is any recognition of the failure of his own efforts to "organize" the streets, or any acknowledgment of the failure of the much-vaunted human advancement programs of the Clinton Administration**, and the myriad welfare programs to alleviate the misery of his brothers.

To the contrary, he would soon call for more and bigger government relief programs, reflecting the Sisyphean liberal belief that there is no problem that can't be really screwed up by pushing more money up the hill of welfare until the system fails under its own weight – only to be tried again by the next generation of unteachables. Ironically, when relief would finally come to his brothers it would result in Obama's first major scandal, one that plagues him to this day with the end result still unknown, as we'll see.

But first things first.

Obama, at 33, moved into Chicago's Hyde Park neighborhood and took a job at the law firm of Miner, Barnhill & Galland because of their focus on civil rights law. And he set about writing his memoirs. Talk about hubris.

One might say Obama was in a hurry. Just not in a hurry to practice at law. In fact, **his career as a lawyer would be measured not in years, or even months, but hours**.

When an opportunity came in 1995 to run for public office, Obama seized it. An Illinois State Senator by the name of Alice Palmer had decided to run for the U.S. Congress, which opened up her old seat. Palmer shared similar liberal views to Obama, and she threw her support behind Obama for her old seat. This is where the story gets messy.

Obama says Palmer agreed that even if she was not successful in her bid for Congress, she would retire from politics. Palmer says her race for Congress fell apart so she wanted her old job back. In this "he said, she said" tussle, Obama was the junior player and disadvantaged by it. He feared getting bumped from a race that, as a liberal, he was likely to win. He was stuck, but in the nick of time, he spied an opening.

Palmer was required by Illinois law to obtain nearly 1,600 petitions to get her name officially on the ballot. She had only 10 days to accomplish this, but she succeeded. Obama immediately challenged the legality of her petitions. Turns out, many of the voters had *printed* their names, instead of *signing* their names as the law required. Palmer tried in vain to obtain affidavits from those who had printed their names, but time ran out on her, and she was forced to withdraw. When the dust settled, Obama was left unopposed in the primary race.

His tactics earned him a reputation for being, like the First Lady in the White House at this time in the 1990s, willing to do whatever it takes to advance in politics.

# A quick study in pay-to-play politics.

With an easy win in the general election, Obama was an Illinois State Senator and what a grand time to be one. The south side of Chicago was undergoing a major development boom. Once blighted areas were experiencing their first waves of gentrification. Large real estate and construction companies were eager to get their hands on the multi-million dollar building contracts being awarded, so they liberally curried favor with the local politicians. Big cash checks flowed into Obama's campaign coffers. One of the real estate developers who actively courted Obama was a Syrian-born political-fixer named Tony Rezko

The two had been social friends for over a decade, with the Rezko's dining out a few times a year with the Obama's. Rezko was not shy about hosting fundraisers for Obama. Then in 2005, the Obama's wanted to purchase property in swank Hyde Park. Michelle, in particular, wanted a good-sized home as a refuge from the public trappings of fame. But the asking price of their dream property was $1.6 million—well out of their range.[43]

What did Obama do?

He did what any man of the people would do. He approached Rezko with the idea of pooling their resources and buying two lots right next to each other—one for the Obama's, one for the Rezko's. Sounded like a fine idea to Rezko. The lots were identically priced for sale by the same owner. But, as reported in *The Chicago Tribune*, **Obama paid $300,000 *under* the asking price for his lot, while Rezko paid *full price* for his adjoining lot. So, did the Rezko's subsidize the purchase of Obama's new property?**

Now that you answered that, ask yourself this: When the Rezko's gave a 10-foot parcel of their land to the Obama's so Barack and Michelle could have a bigger yard, was that just a display of the grand charity that the Rezko's show in their life?

Did we mention that Rezko had been indicted *just months before* on federal fraud charges?

Anyone reading the newspaper knew of the indictment. Rezko was charged with fraud, attempted extortion, money laundering, and aiding bribery. Seems Rezko had tried to extort millions of dollars from firms attempting to do business with the teachers' pension board and state hospital regulatory panel. Prosecutors say Rezko used his influence to get friends onto government boards. Then those friends demanded nearly $6 million in kickbacks from contractors in exchange for okaying building projects.

And did we mention that the Obama campaign reported only $160,000 of the campaign contributions received from Rezko? Another $90,000 in contributions were not reported. Not until Chicago newspapers began checking the election records and noting "the discrepancy." But calling $90,000 a discrepancy is like calling politicians clean—it don't wash. A political campaign can misplace $90 or even $900 but not $90,000. Why Obama did not report this contribution is unknown.

In the federal trial against Rezko, **prosecutors said that some of Rezko's extortion money ended up in Obama's campaign coffers**. But the details of the prosecutor's investigation have been sealed—protecting Obama from further inquiries, for now.

This whole episode didn't come to light after years of faithful service in public office. This came to the public's attention only *two years* into Obama's political career, raising serious questions about Obama's judgment, and his ethical compass.

Obama has admitted that the whole affair stunk. But he only began holding his nose when the story became public, and people began asking if Obama was the kind of politician who would cast aside his professed sense of ethics for personal financial gain.

When he finally spoke out, Obama admitted to the *Chicago Sun-Times* that his actions were *"boneheaded,"* because they gave *"the appearance of impropriety … this is an area where I can see sort of a lapse in judgment."*

Oh really?

Obama has since donated that money to charity, as is the custom of politicians who get caught with dirty money.

Does this episode suggest Obama is the kind of politician who can be bought? If it looks like a duck, and quacks like a duck … it might be Obama. Obama was well-familiar with Rezko's shady reputation, and ought to have avoided all appearance of impropriety.

**What has Rezko received in return for his generosity?** That information may still come out, but for now the principal legal action against Rezko has concluded. In June 2008, Rezko was found guilty on 16 of 24 counts of fraud and political corruption by a Chicago jury. Within hours of the verdict in federal court, Obama released a statement saying he was *"saddened"* by Rezko's conviction and added:

*"This isn't the Tony Rezko I knew."*

Remember this line of Obama's—we will hear its familiar refrain over and over in the pages to come:

*"This isn't the Jeremiah Wright I knew."*

*"This isn't the William Ayres I knew."*

*"This isn't the Michael Pfleger I knew."*

*"This isn't the George Soros I knew."*

*"This isn't the Reverend Moss I knew."*

*"This isn't the Louis Farrakhan I knew."*

At one point, we wonder if there is anybody in Obama's past who can be trotted out in public without the assistance of a parole officer or an apologist?

Incidentally, if the name Tony Rezko sounds familiar to you, perhaps it is because Obama is not the first politician Rezko has tried to buy. Chicago prosecutors have linked Rezko's codefendants to the Clinton fundraising, though it is unclear whether any of the campaign contributions were illegal.

Writing in *The Conservative Voice,* Tom Fitton has drawn the parallel to another "property for political access" land deal in our political lexicon:

> *Clinton's came into the White House despite evidence of their shady real estate dealings in Arkansas, a scandal known as Whitewater, setting the tone for what would be the most corrupt presidency in our nation's history. Is this Rezko land deal Barack Obama's Whitewater? Let's find out sooner than later.*

## Not just business sleaze, but racial sleaze.

If Tony Rezko is the face of business sleaze in Chicago, Jesse Jackson has long been the face of racial sleaze. For decades his Rainbow/PUSH organization has shaken-down businesses and put-down fellow blacks, all in service of Jackson's oversized ego and bank account.

When Obama moved into Hyde Park, just down the street from Jackson, Obama had the opportunity to keep relations cordial but at arm's length. In this way, he could have lent added credibility to his "new politics."

But from the very beginning, **Jesse Jackson signed-on as an advisor to Obama, informally at first and then in an official capacity**. In fact, Michelle Obama arranged their initial meeting, in hopes of fast-tracking her husband in Chicago's black network. Michelle had grown up on Chicago's South Side with Jackson's daughter, and had often baby-sat young Jesse Jr.

The families have become close. Jesse Jackson can be counted on to bring his racial sleaze-mongering into an Obama White House.

# 5. Does Obama's Rhetoric Sync With His Policy Positions?

For all his earnestness and vigor, Obama didn't set the Illinois state legislature on fire. Recalls his media advisor, Dan Shomon:

> The first few years he was thought of as intelligent, thoughtful, bright. But he certainly wasn't considered to be a major player.[44]

In his first three years, Obama introduced 116 bills, and 25 of them became law. It wasn't a terribly bad pace for a rookie, and his programs did help the constituents who sent him to Springfield. As the years passed, however, he grew more risk averse.

After eight years **Obama was on record as having voted "Present" a remarkable 130 times. Present? Isn't that what children say in school when the teacher takes attendance**, not what a grown-up does to avoid taking definitive stands on important issues?

Looking back, it would be easy to conclude that Obama already had his sights set on the presidency and that he wanted to take no more controversial positions than absolutely necessary, offering a smaller target for the arrows of future opponents. Right or wrong, Obama's voting record as an Illinois State Senator brings into clear focus the liberal philosophy that guides his politics.

Here are the key votes from Obama's time in Springfield:

## On Abortion

*SB 230 (1997)* Would outlaw partial-birth abortion except when necessary to save the life of a mother. Would make performance of this procedure a Class 4 felony for the physician.

> **Obama: NO, there should be no restrictions on abortions.**

*SB 1661 (2002)* Would call for prosecution of physicians if a child is born alive after an abortion and the living child is later neglected.

> **Obama: NO, physicians should not be responsible if an abortion fails and the child lives.**

Not surprisingly, when Obama later ran for U.S. Senate, he received almost $42,000 in campaign contributions from abortion activists.[45] Obama has a gift for portraying himself as an even-handed politician who is inspired by traditional religious values. But he has worked hard to earn a 100% rating from NARAL Pro-Choice America—which is about as far away from traditional religious values as it gets.

## *On Crime*

*SB 381 (1997)* Would require prisoners to pay the court costs if they launch a lawsuit against the state that is found to be "frivolous."

> **Obama: NO, incarcerated felons should be able to sue the state, using lawyers paid-for by taxpayer dollars.**

*SB 485 (1999)* Would stop convicted sexual predators from getting early paroles for "good time" served.

> **Obama: NO, let sexual predators out of jail as fast as possible.** (Note: Obama was the only Senator to vote "no" on this measure)

In 1999, Illinois Governor George Ryan was pushing the Safe Neighborhoods Act as a way to crack down on crime. Obama's district was being ravaged by crime, and so Obama supported the bill. But when it came to a vote, Obama was vacationing with his family in Hawaii. He was stuck. If he left the family vacation early, he would anger Michelle who was tired of having an absentee husband. They were, Obama has written, "barely on speaking terms." So Obama stayed in Hawaii and missed the vote. Even then, Obama could envision a political ad in his future: Obama sipping a tropical drink on Waikiki while an anti-crime bill fails to get enough votes, and Chicago suffers the highest murder rate since Al Capone.

## On Unions

*HB 3396 (2003)* Would make it easier for unions to organize workers by getting around the "secret ballot" approach that has long protected workers.

> **Obama: YES, unions should be stronger.** (Note: Obama is sponsoring similar legislation in the U.S. Senate to apply nationwide.)

*SB 230 (2003)* Gives teachers a 6-year leave of absence if they take a job strengthening the teachers' union.

> **Obama: YES, unions should be stronger even if children suffer the loss of teachers.**

*SB 1070 (2003)* Allows college teaching assistants to join a union.

> **Obama: YES, unions should be stronger, all votes consistent with Obama's years spent organizing the community and avoiding business economics.**

## On Child Protection

*SB 609 (2001)* Would forbid "adult" stores from locating within 1,000 feet of any school, public park, church, day-care facility, mobile home park, or residential area.

> **Obama: PRESENT, in other words, not willing to take
> a stand. If a porno shop wants to open up across
> from a day-care facility, then Obama says, let it!**

*HB 1812 (1999)* Would require schools to filter pornography from
school computers.

> **Obama: NO, let the young kids be exposed to all the
> filth they want. He believes it tramples on the First
> Amendment!**

## On Taxes

*SB 1075 (1999)* Would give an income tax credit to parents for
their children's education expenses up to $500 per family.

> **Obama: NO, we have adequate taxpayer-supported
> public schools, though I'm not sending my two girls to
> those dumps.**

*SB 1725 (2003)* Would restore the Illinois Estate Tax.

> **Obama: YES, why should families pass their wealth from
> one generation to the next?**

*SB 1733 (2003)* Would tax the purchase of natural gas from outside
Illinois.

> **Obama: YES, fuel prices aren't high enough yet, and
> we politicians need to find spending money wherever
> we can.**

## On Homosexual Rights

*SB 228 (1997)* Would require the government, if it gives any
special benefits to homosexual couples, to give equal benefits to
heterosexual couples.

**Obama: NO, with no explanation. (He couldn't possibly believe that reverse discrimination is acceptable. So he must have been kowtowing to the gay lobby.)**

Indeed, in 2004 when he was running for U.S. Senate, Obama wrote to the *Windy City Times*, a gay publication:

*I opposed DOMA [the Defense of Marriage Act] in 1996. It should be repealed, and I will vote for its repeal on the Senate floor… I will also oppose any proposal to amend the U.S. Constitution to ban gays and lesbians from marrying.*

He also pledged to work to "expand adoption rights" for same-sex couples.

## On Drugs

*SB 880 (2003)* Would allow the purchase of 10 hypodermic needles from a pharmacy without a prescription.
**Obama: YES, why not 20 needles?**

*HB 2000 (4659)* Would establish a zero-tolerance drug-testing policy for Department of Corrections Employees.
**Obama: PRESENT, don't want to offend the prison guards, and don't want to appear soft on crime, so I'll just sit on my hands.**

## On Business

Between 1999 and 2001, three bills came to the Senate floor to help businesses cope with the rising costs and endless paperwork involved in employee insurance programs. Obama voted against all three bills, offering no help to employers.[46]

*SB 796 (2003)* Would increase the Illinois minimum wage from $5.15 to $6.50 per hour.

> **Obama: YES, workers should be paid more even if businesses become uncompetitive as a result, and they go out of business.**

## On Healthcare

Voted to require the state to provide universal healthcare for all, to be funded with money taken from tobacco companies. And Obama added this language to the bill:

> *Healthcare is an essential safeguard of human life and dignity, and there is an obligation for society to ensure that every person is able to realize that right."*

## Establishing his strong liberal credentials.

At this stage, early in his political career, Obama appeared to be every bit the biracial George McGovern, offering the same big government liberalism pushed by the Left since the Great Society. However, he was not always shy about criticizing his fellow black leaders or their legislative agendas. And he did not always follow the black caucus talking points. In fact, Obama's temper raged more than once—and especially at fellow Senator Rickey Hendon who was a flamboyant type and knew how to get under Obama's skin.

At least once, the two men reportedly came to fisticuffs. Obama had just voted against taxpayer goodies for Hendon's district. Apparently, Obama made a mistake—he actually voted *against* a spending proposal. Imagine that! So, reverting to type, Obama asked that the record reflect a misvote. At that, Hendon accused Obama of duplicity. Abruptly, the two were in each other's faces on the Senate floor, shouting at each other. As biographer David Mendell describes:

*They took their disagreement to a side room, and a witness said that Obama had to be physically restrained ... Hendon won't discuss the altercation, except to confirm that it occurred.*[47]

But arguing down small-time lawmakers was not the future Obama had in mind for himself. And as his first term came to an end, those ambitions would lead to a giant political miscalculation.

Obama had been eyeing the Mayor's job, figuring that would be the next step in his political ascendancy. But while Obama had been away at Harvard, Mayor Richard M. Daley had been making peace with the black community, building a massive political army, and Daley was now considered unbeatable.

So Obama looked to the U.S. Congress, deciding to challenge Representative Bobby Rush in the 2000 Democratic Primary. To Obama, Bobby Rush looked vulnerable; he hadn't accomplished anything of note during his tenure in Washington. But what Rush did have going for him was black celebrity status. He had been a Black Panther in the 1960s—what else did voters on the South Side need to know?

When Obama entered the race, flashing his Harvard credentials, a lot of black people thought him a sellout, a fancy boy, a toady for the "Hyde Park mafia." Obama tried to remind voters that he had been active in the poor neighborhoods. But his community service couldn't hold a candle to being a former Black Panther. Not with this crowd.

Then just a few months before the primary, Bobby Rush's son was gunned down in what police called a drug deal gone sour. The outpouring of support for Rush was overwhelming, and Obama knew he was going down in defeat. In the final weeks of the campaign, Bobby Rush **portrayed Obama as a young piker who had the gall to ask voters to send him to Washington. *"Just what's he done?"*** Rush asked. *"What's he done?"* The message hit home with voters. Obama lost by 30 points.

It's safe to say, Obama learned some lessons. As he licked his wounds and began meeting with his handlers in Chicago and on the national scene, Obama began also to refashion a new mask for himself. His stump speeches included talk of a *"new politics"* from a *"change agent"* working with a *"higher ethical bar."*

It was savvy positioning for a politician now eyeing the U.S. Senate. Voters were tired of the baby-boomer in-fighting and strident partisanship found at all levels of government. If young Obama could offer a fresh view or a new approach, voters might bite. So it is doubly interesting that reporters from the *Chicago Tribune* covering the rebirth of Obama had this to report:

> *State Sen. Barack Obama claims the mantle of a reformer, but early last month the Democratic U.S. Senate candidate spent $17,191 in state taxpayer money on a mailer that had the look and feel of a campaign flier. The mailing went out just days before a new ban on the pre-election dissemination of such state-paid constituent newsletters went into effect, part of a package of ethics reforms that Obama takes credit for getting passed.*

New politics? Sounds more like politicians using taxpayer money to get themselves reelected. Not much new in that.

Whether new politician or old, in his Senate race, Obama would become the luckiest politician of modern times.

In the Democratic primary, there were seven candidates vying for the nomination. Not one of them ran a negative TV ad. The strongest contender flamed out when *someone* leaked his divorce file to the media painting a very unflattering picture of the man. Obama went on to sweep the primary election.

Obama's Republican opponent in the general election, co-incidentally, also was the victim of a divorce scandal. Scrambling fast, the Republicans chose as a backup candidate, Alan Keyes, a man who had never lived in Illinois, and who delivered a strong conservative message.

## Does Obama's Rhetoric Sync with His Policy Positions?

With plenty of financial backing, Obama ran a series of television ads shouting, *"Yes, we can."* Everyone could agree with this message and make it their own. Yes, a politician like Obama could make life better. Yes, a black man could win a U.S. Senate seat. Yes, we can all be heard. To those who thought it impossible to change Washington, Obama corrected, *"Yes, we can."*

Obama won handily in November. Obama himself had to admit:

> *There was no point in denying my almost spooky good fortune. I was an outlier, a freak; to political insiders, my victory proved nothing.*[48]

Obama was right. He would arrive in Washington having never been truly tested by a credible opponent, having never seen his ideas challenged in the political marketplace. That would come soon enough. But before Washington, Obama would give a speech that would transform modern politics.

# 6. How Was The "Cult Of Obama" Manufactured?

## "I'm LeBron, baby!"

Obama first came onto the national radar at the Democratic National Convention in July 2004. Democrats assembled in the Fleet Center in Boston heard Obama deliver one of the finest keynote speeches in the party's history. There was not a dry eye as Obama introduced his "new politics" with such passion and eloquence that even conservative commentators were moved by the oration.

Obama's biographer David Mendell had talked with Obama just before the speech and he could see that Obama was raring to go. *"I'm LeBron, baby!"* Obama exclaimed, referring to LeBron James, the basketball phenom. *"I can play on this level. I got some game."*

Up on the podium, Obama made everyone believe in an America of good-hearted people, a nation more unified than divided, an America where everyone shares the twin goals of freedom and opportunity for all:

> There's not a liberal America and a conservative America—there's the United States of America.

Obama offered himself as the sum of many yearnings. Here, in one man, was the long-awaited antidote to the splintered, senselessly partisan politics of Washington.

Here in one man was the blend of pragmatism and hope that this country needs to find the way to a better tomorrow.

Here at last was the perfect blend of confidence, character, and vision …all in one man. More powerful than a conservative's tax break, faster than a speeding rumor, able to leap the truth in a single bound—*ObamaMan!*

America had not heard a story like Obama's. A mother who was white and from Kansas, a father who was black and from Kenya. Raised in Hawaii and Indonesia, taught Muslim and Christian virtues. Married to a black girl from the South Side of Chicago, where he had worked to organize the poor. Onto the country's finest law school, and then to that school's highest ranks of individual achievement as President of the Harvard Law Review. And here he was, in Boston, offering himself as an embodiment of the American dream, where people of all races, beliefs and values could join together to make the republic whole again, indivisible.

It was a great story. And most of it true…

## Playing the sex appeal for all its worth.

Presenting such an attractive package to a political party that was desperate for honest, or at least not completely dishonest leadership, it was inevitable that "Obama" and "Messiah" would begin appearing in the same sentence, in total seriousness.

At the Art Institute of Chicago, a student created a statue of "Obama as Jesus," complete with a neon halo and arms lifted to the heavens.

The liberal blogger known as Wonkette was over the top in expressing what a lot of young people felt:

> He is a rock star! He hasn't gone old for us! Uh, he hasn't developed into some joke that he tells over and over! He's the neeeew, vaguely exotic foreign exchange student! He's the sexiest of the new people… I actually was at a cocktail party where Barack was! Talk about sexy! He's so young! It's the first blush … Obama can do no wrong! Sexy! Sexy! Sexy![49]

Only slightly less restrained, Chicago magazines put Obama atop the list of politicians who had the "it" factor. The *Sun-Times* gushed:

> The first African-American President of the Harvard Law Review has a movie-star smile and more than a little

*mystique. Also, we just like to say his name. We are considering taking it as a mantra.*

A political cartoon came out with a starry-eyed woman holding a sign: DATED DEAN, MARRIED KERRY, LUST FOR OBAMA.

New Hampshire governor John Lynch had booked the Rolling Stones for a big fundraiser. But in what may be a first in political and entertainment history, Mick Jagger and the Stones were cancelled. Obama could sell more tickets.

A Washington political consultant took the Chicago sculptor a step further, labeling Obama the "Black Jesus." Even Obama's drug use as a teenager was turned to his advantage. Asked about smoking pot by Jay Leno, Obama quipped, *"I inhaled; that was the point."* That earned a collective laugh from late-night viewers across America.

At last, some honesty.

Obama's appeal wasn't limited to hormonal babes and gawkers. He could even wow conservatives. David Wilhelm, an Obama advisor tells how:

> *[Obama] has the whole venture capital industry here in Chicago, nothing but Republicans, thinking he is their champion.*

They think this because they hear what they want to hear in his words. With his reasonable tone and studied thoughtfulness, his ingenious lack of specificity, his self-deprecating sense of humor, it all combines to create a cotton-candy light-headedness.

Ronald Reagan was the last national politician to speak as well as Obama. That Reagan took actual positions in his speeches mattered not to Obama's adoring fans. Obama has mounted a plausible campaign for the presidency based on personal magnetism—of which he has an abundance. **Michael Reagan calls him "the Halle Berry of politics." Who doesn't want to watch?**

Make no mistake, having the "it" factor can pay dividends.

Psychologists who study these things tell us that good-looking people are treated better than bad-looking people. Studies show that a *handsome* man enjoys a six to ten point edge over a *plain* rival. Make no mistake, "looks" are going to matter in this election.

Ironically, Obama has had trouble speaking away from the Teleprompter. At a campaign news conference, he said, "uh" 144 times in eleven minutes. As Judge Judy says, "Uh, is not an answer." This may be why he is avoiding having town hall meetings with John McCain.

## Being whatever you desire in a politician.

The columnist Mac Johnson has written of Obama:

*[Obama] is like a small, shiny object. The easily fascinated can stare deeply into his blank sheen and see ... their own reflections. He can be anything to anyone because he is nothing in particular. Yet listening to the left-stream media, one would have to conclude that the man is a multifaceted miracle. He's a moderate. He's a third way. He's demographic fusion cuisine. He's a floor wax. He's a desert topping. He's everything you'd hoped for and whatever you need.*

It means little that only a handful of close supporters can name even a single one of Obama's legislative accomplishments, Democrats are in love. They tend to do that, on the first date. While Republicans tend to nominate their party's seasoned senior statesmen, Democrats get swept away right away. Then they find themselves stuck with the guy, wearing his ring. Night after night of hearing the same wondrous platitudes, they begin wondering what they initially found so inspiring.

Democrats are excited about how Obama overcame great adversity and in the face of oppression, succeeded grandly. Democrats love this kind of stuff, initially anyway. But then the nagging questions begin.  Like this one, "What great oppression has Obama really overcome?"

- Is it the oppression of growing up on the beaches of Hawaii?

- Is it the oppression of affirmative action quotas that eased him into Columbia and Harvard Law?

- Is it the oppression of his funny name and big ears? Surely the kids must have teased the heck out of him.

If Obama is to face any oppression in the future, it will probably come from people who wonder when he's going to take his eloquent oration for "change" into actual policies that create actual change in actual people's lives.

## What "change" has Obama brought to the U.S. Senate?

**It's a fair question to ask when...**  Obama had served only one year in the U.S. Senate when he decided to run for President.  From that point onward, Obama was full throttle ahead, next stop 1600 Pennsylvania Avenue.  That left little time for the inconvenient details of the job the good people of Illinois elected him to.

**It's a fair question to ask when...** As a Democrat, Obama was in the minority in the Senate and would have to work with Republicans across the aisle to get legislation passed. Working "across the aisle" would mean delivering on his promise to be a unifier.  So how much unifying went down?  Obama passed exactly one substantial piece of legislation, and voted lockstep with the Democratic leadership 95% of the time.[50]

**It's a fair question to ask when...**  Part of the plan to give Obama stature and bearing on the global stage required a trip to Africa. It would be a fact-finding mission, a chance to visit his relatives in Kenya, and, his advisers hoped, a public relations coup.

**Yes, it's a fair question to ask what "change" Obama brought to the Senate. He was too busy for that.**

There was one endeavor Obama committed himself to in Washington: Earmarks. You know, those little last minute spending requests congressional representatives add to bills for the folks back home. Only in Obama's case, the recipients of his largesse were very close to home.

In 2006, Obama requested an earmark of $1 million for the University of Chicago Hospital. Any idea which woman in Obama's life holds the title of Vice President for Community Affairs at that hospital? That's right, Michelle Obama!

Wasting no time in leaping to her defense, *The New York Times* proclaimed that Michelle had never lobbied Barack on behalf of her employer for the $1 million. How did they know this? Did they bug the couple's bedroom? However The Times learned that Barack and Michelle didn't talk about the million dollars he inserted into the spending bill, the hospital was certainly pleased he did it. And Michelle, who had been earning $122,000 before her husband became a Senator, saw her salary leap to $317,000 after he took office. Is this merely a coincidence?

Beyond all the financial gain that Obama's political position has brought to his family, what have Obama's Senate votes done for his constituents in Illinois and the rest of the country?

## *On National Defense*

Obama has been consistent in his votes on national security—making it easy to judge the philosophy that guides him in this area:

- When MoveOn.org launched the most despicable attack on an American General in the history of this country, asking in full page ads if General Petraeus was "General Betray Us," every respectable politician denounced the ad and its chicanery. But one politician chose to "be otherwise detained" during the vote. Obama chose to hide from that vote ... because Obama didn't want to upset the radical leftist anti-war activists.

- Believing that the due process rights of Islamofascists who attacked America are more important than aggressively waging the war on terrorism, Obama voted to give a whole package of additional due process rights to enemy insurgents in U.S. custody.

- A key ally in tracking down terrorists is the phone companies. By working with these phone companies, the government can wiretap calls and often intercept terrorist activity before it's too late. Obama says this practice is wrong. He believes that lawyers should be able to sue phone companies for participating in terrorist stings.

- On the Iraq War, Obama did not vote to authorize the war because he was not a Senator until 2004. However, he has consistently denounced the war effort, calling it a distraction from the real focus which should be Afghanistan, calling for an immediate but gradual withdrawal of troops, leaving behind only a small number to conduct counterterrorism operations and protect diplomats. Obama voted 15 times to limit funding, impose deadlines for troop withdrawal, and restrict combat activities.

- When the Congress called on President Bush to attempt to lessen Iranian influence on Iraq, and to designate the Iranian revolutionary guard as a terrorist organization, Obama voted against the measure.

- He has shown a get tough attitude in only one trouble spot—Barack Obama would strike Al Qaeda in northwest Pakistan if we had actionable intelligence. He has said he believes that we are playing to Osama bin Laden's game plan for winning a war from a cave, and that Al Qaeda is stronger than before thanks to the Bush doctrine. This is a dubious claim at best, since we have not been successfully attacked since 9/11. This would widen the war to a new country.

## On Global Poverty

Obama has sponsored the Global Poverty Act (S.2433) that would commit an estimated $845 billion of U.S. taxpayer money to foreign poverty-fighting programs.

This would be the biggest transfer of wealth out of the country in our long history. It would fall into the hands of brutal ruling juntas, corrupt aid workers, and occasionally, people who need it. This legislation is an overt act to "make them like us," when the reason we are, or are not, liked overseas cannot be changed with boxes of rice powder dropped from C-5 transports.

It has been said, by John Bunyan, that a hypocrite is a saint abroad and a devil at home. In this case, Obama fits the description.

## On Unions

Obama has curried additional favor with the labor unions by trying to force employees of the Homeland Security Department to unionize. He supports workers' rights to organize and strike and would give all public safety officers new collective bargaining rights. He was a chief cosponsor of IL ENDA, a bill increasing homosexual job protections against discrimination. He wants to make the minimum wage higher through regular increases. He sponsored a bill allowing an Air Traffic Controller's Union.

- He voted NO on terminating legal challenges to English-only job rules. (March 2008)

- He voted YES on restricting employer interference in union organizing. (June 2007)

- He voted YES on increasing minimum wage to $7.25. (February 2007)

## *On Gun Control Legislation*

Obama is on record as favoring outlawing all handguns, a vote he insists was the result of a rogue aide filling out a questionnaire. But Obama's own handwritten notes were found on the questionnaire, once again calling into question his version of the truth.

After the Supreme Court decision on the right to bear arms in Washington DC, he attempted to switch sides, but he previously supported DC's gun ban.

He endorsed Illinois' handgun ban. He says he respects the Second Amendment, but supports local gun bans.

In 2000, he cosponsored a bill to limit purchases to one gun a month.

He believes Bush erred in failing to renew the assault weapons ban, and would ban semi-automatics.

He also voted NO on prohibiting lawsuits against gun manufacturers. (July 2005)

## *On the Supreme Court*

When John Roberts was nominated to the post of Chief Justice, 78 Senators voted to confirm the man the American Bar Association called *"well qualified,"* and a justice most people agree has been a voice of reason and restraint on the high bench. Only 22 of the most liberal Senators, including Obama, voted against Roberts. (September 2005)

This would be the easiest crossing-of-the aisle action Obama could have made to step-lively in his post-partisanship crusade. But he couldn't find the way.

He also voted NO on confirming Samuel Alito as Supreme Court Justice. (January 2006)

## *On Immigration*

Obama supported a big immigration package that would give illegal immigrants a free pass to citizenship. He supports the DREAM Act for the children of illegal immigrants. He does not believe we have allocated enough for the healthcare of illegal immigrants. He does not think that illegal immigrants should be able to work, but that they should have a path to citizenship. He would not deputize Americans to turn in illegal immigrants. He supports government services provided in Spanish and granting driver's licenses to illegal immigrants. He would extend welfare and Medicaid to immigrants and provide funding for social services for noncitizens.

- *He voted YES on continuing federal funds for declared "sanctuary cities." (March 2008)*

- *He voted YES on comprehensive immigration reform. (June 2007)*

- *He voted YES on establishing a Guest Worker program. (May 2006)*

- *He voted YES on allowing illegal aliens to participate in Social Security. (May 2006)*

- *He voted YES on giving Guest Workers a path to citizenship. (May 2006)*

## *On English as the Official Language of the US Government*

Obama voted against declaring English the official language of the U.S. Government. (June 2007) When asked to explain his vote, he is rumored to have muttered something in Swahili. Perhaps he would have us speak an amalgam of Chinese, Spanish, and English in Washington. Chipanglish, anyone?

## *On Abortion*

Obama is rated a perfect 100% by the National Abortion Rights Action League on pro-choice votes in 2005, 2006 and 2007, and rated 0% by the National Right to Life.

He believes the Constitution is a living document and is opposed to strict constructionism. He thinks moral arguments from pro-lifers are counterproductive. He supports Roe v. Wade and will protect a "woman's right to choose."

- He voted NO on defining unborn child as eligible for SCHIP. (March 2008)

- He voted NO on prohibiting minors crossing state lines for abortion. (March 2008)

- He voted against banning partial birth abortion. (October 2007)

- He voted YES on expanding research to more embryonic stem cell lines. (April 2007)

- He voted NO on notifying parents of minors who get out-of-state abortions. (July 2006)

- He voted YES on $100M to reduce teen pregnancy by education & contraceptives. (March 2005)

- He sponsored legislation to provide contraceptives for low-income. (May 2006)

## *On the Budget & Economy*

Obama plans to eliminate the Bush tax cuts and will raise $150 billion with this tax increase. He rejects a free market vision of government, and believes that Bush's economic policies are not working. He voted NO on $40 billion in federal spending reductions. (December 2005)

## On Affirmative Action

Obama would apply affirmative action to poor white college applicants, and include class-based affirmative action with race-based. He supports affirmative action in colleges and government and would re-introduce the Equal Rights Amendment. He is rated 100% by the NAACP.

## On Homosexual Rights

Obama believes that being gay or lesbian is not a choice, and that decisions about marriage should be left to the states. He sees homosexuality as no more immoral than heterosexuality, and is okay with exposing 6-year-olds to gay couples. He views the gay rights movement somewhat like the civil rights movement. He supports health benefits for gay civil partners. He says he personally opposes gay marriage but supports the states' right to allow it. He actively supports civil unions. He would include sexual orientation in anti-discrimination laws. He is rated 89% by the HRC which indicates a pro-gay-rights stance. He voted NO on constitutional ban of same-sex marriage. (June 2006)

## On Crime

Obama would ban racial profiling and eliminate disparities in sentencing. He would increase the size of the Justice Departments Civil Rights Division and aggressively enforce anti-discrimination laws. He pushed an Illinois bill to videotape all capital interrogations. He does not believe there should be any extra penalty for gang association, and thinks that the death penalty is wrong in many cases because of its disproportionate impact on black Americans.

## On Drugs

Obama supports needle exchange programs. He is not the first candidate to use drugs (cocaine and marijuana), but is probably the first to brag about it. He smokes cigarettes, and says he understands why youngsters want to use drugs.

## On Education

Obama would give $4,000 in college tuition for 100 hours of public service a year, and would put billions of dollars into early childhood education. He would pay "master teachers" extra, but only with the buy-in from teachers. He wants to create incentives to hire a million teachers over next decade. He believes that sex education is needed to help children discuss molestation. He would provide free public college for any student with B-average. Lastly, he voted to shift $11 billion from corporate deductions to education.

## On Energy & Oil

Obama would raise automobile fuel efficiency standards to 40 mpg to reduce long-term gasoline demand, and push to reduce carbon emissions by 80% by 2050. He believes in aggressively addressing climate change, and supports cap-and-trade on carbon emissions. He does not believe we should increase domestic drilling. He calls our use of oil an "addiction."

- He voted Yes for the tax credit for installing E85 ethanol at gas stations. (February 2008)

- He voted YES on removing oil & gas exploration subsidies. (June 2007)

- He voted YES on factoring global warming into federal project planning. (May 2007)

- He voted YES on disallowing an oil leasing program in the Arctic National Wildlife Refuge. (November 2005)

- He voted YES on banning drilling in the Arctic National Wildlife Refuge. (March 2005)

- He sponsored a bill for tax credit for providing 85% ethanol gas. (April 2005)

## *On Free Trade*

Obama believes NAFTA needs to be amended.

- He voted YES on a free trade agreement with Oman. (June 2006)

- He voted NO on implementing CAFTA for Central America free-trade. (July 2005)

## On Government Reform

On campaign finance reform Obama believes that money is the original sin in politics. He supports reduced cost of TV ads for candidates, and even has supported public financing for campaigns with free television and radio time. He is okay with taking $5 donations from drug company employees. He opposes taking money from lobbyists, but takes them from bundlers who lobby and from lobbyist's spouses. He sponsored a resolution rejecting photo ID for voting. (September 2005)

## *On Healthcare*

Obama supports end-of-life self-medication or suicide, but he says he opposes euthanasia. Obama supports condom distribution to deal with AIDS, and he believes that homophobia prevents people from talking about HIV/AIDS. He would increase funding for AIDS treatment and prevention.

He believes he can take on insurance companies to drive down healthcare costs. Obama would turn no one away with illness or a pre-existing condition. His definition of Universal Healthcare is anyone who wants it can get it. He supports mandating that we have insurance. Obama supported a single-payer system at one point, but shifted his position in the campaign. He says we need political will to accomplish universal coverage, and does not believe that the market alone can solve our problems. He believes that healthcare is a right, not a privilege.

## On Social Security

Obama would raise the $97,000 cap on payroll tax exempting earnings under $250,000 (which amounts to a $1.3 trillion dollar tax increase). He would stop any efforts to privatize Social Security, and he believes that the wealthy should pay more of the Social Security payroll tax.

## On Tax Reform

Obama would raise the capital gains tax, not for revenue, even it resulted in less government revenue, but "for fairness." He is not bashful about it, the wealthy will pay more taxes if he is elected. He would restore a progressive tax and close loopholes. He would reduce the Bush tax cuts to pay for healthcare and other programs, and believes that they helped corporations but not middle class. He believes that the last thing we need now is a permanent tax cut.

- He voted YES to increase the tax rate of people earning over $1 million. (March 2008)

- He voted NO on allowing AMT reduction without budget offset. (March 2008)

- He voted NO on raising the Death Tax exemption to $5 million from $1 million. (February 2008)

- He voted NO on repealing the Alternative Minimum Tax. (March 2007)

- He voted NO on raising estate tax exemption to $5 million. (March 2007)

- He voted NO on supporting permanence of estate tax cuts. (August 2006)

- He voted NO on permanently repealing the `death tax`. (June 2006)

- He voted NO on retaining reduced taxes on capital gains and dividends. (February 2006)

- He voted NO on extending the tax cuts on capital gains and dividends. (November 2005)

Obama wants voters to believe he will bring "change" to Washington. Yet he hasn't tried very hard to bring change when he is in Washington.  Of the 245 votes that came to the Senate floor as tracked by VoteSmart.org, Obama showed up to vote on only 116—he missed more votes than he cast. One of the reasons for this was that he was busy building his foreign policy credentials in Africa...

# New revelations on Obama's African tour.

When Obama journeyed to Africa for a five-nation tour in his first year in the Senate, his handlers had high hopes for him. They knew he had zero foreign policy experience, and expected that to be a liability in a Presidential election in a time of war.

The trip was by all accounts a phenomenal success. In his homeland of Kenya, Obama was mobbed by frenzied Africans eager to lay hands on one of their own. Town leaders feted him at every stop. The media dutifully chronicled the trip of an America hero.

Only one thing may have been missing. The truth.

As we reported in Chapter 1, Obama's ancestors were indeed slave merchants. **At a time in America when the Republican Party was fighting for emancipation, Obama's forbearers were still shackling the wrists of Negroes.**

It's not fair to judge Obama by his ancestors, just as it's not fair to judge today's Democratic Party for its deep historic ties to the KKK. But it is important to be honest about some things. Such as race.

## Obama announces for the Presidency.

After Africa, Obama began talking with his handlers about seriously running for President as early as 2008. First, he spoke with Michelle, then Jeremiah Wright and Jesse Jackson, then the big money people who could make it happen. **The reception he had received in Africa had been so genuinely intoxicating to the junior Senator; he felt that a tide of history was pushing him in just one direction.**

So it was, just a few months later before a crowd of 17,000 supporters on a blustery cold day outside the Old State Capitol in Springfield that Obama announced his candidacy. This is where Abraham Lincoln had delivered his famous "House Divided" antislavery speech in 1858. Obama drew on the powerful historic symbolism of the venue:

> *The life of a tall, gangly, self-made Springfield lawyer tells us that a different future is possible. He tells us that there is power in words. He tells us that there is power in conviction, that beneath all the differences of race and region, faith and station, we are one people. He tells us that there is power in hope.*

## Does Obama's Rhetoric Sync with His Policy Positions?

To his 17,000 supporters in Springfield, and to millions more watching on TV, that historic day would be a defining moment in their lives. The passing of a torch to a new generation. That Obama had gone to Washington and so far accomplished nothing—didn't matter. That his speeches offered little more than feel-good platitudes—didn't matter. His supporters were ready to march.

Across the land they would march, legions of supporters carrying signs and posters, moving to the call and response of *"Fired Up," "Ready to Go,"* and the chant of *"Obama/08/Be a part of something great!"* Shopkeepers and pedestrians applauded wherever they marched.

# II. Create the "Look" Democrats Crave, but...

When Obama locked-in the delegates required to secure the Democratic nomination, the real work began behind the scenes. Obama's handlers in New York and Hollywood now had to package him for the general electorate—a very different assignment, in their view. In this next chapter, we see how they approached their historic task.

# 7. A Pigment Of His Imagination

Whatever course of events led Obama to boldly proclaim that *"the old labels don't matter anymore,"* one wonders who he thinks he's fooling?

In fact, labels such as *liberal*, *conservative* and *radical* can be very useful. Labels don't tell us everything, of course. And they can be misleading to those who never bother to dig any deeper. But as a place to begin, labels matter greatly. Labels tell us how a candidate is likely to approach an issue that is important to us—whether it be free trade, national defense, or abortion.

Clearly Obama's attempt to sell himself as a post-label, post-partisan, post-ideological politician is an attempt to game the system and fool half the voters, plus one.

## Obama would be the second least-prepared President ever.

Obama's supporters claim that *"experience doesn't matter."* They have to claim that. Their candidate is the second least-prepared individual ever to seek the presidency. If you look at every man who has held the office of President in the last 100 years, you cannot find one with less experience than Obama.

We speak of the last 100 years because Lincoln came into the White House having been only a one-term Congressman and a railroad lawyer. But Lincoln didn't try to sell some amorphous notion of "change" while leaving unsaid what kind of change he meant. No, he not only intended to hold a great nation together as one union, he was willing to stake his life on that goal. That was his singular vision, made clear at every campaign stop. Was he savvy enough to know that by holding out certain carrots, specific forms of change – the Emancipation Proclamation comes to mind – he could bend public and political opinion toward his goal? Certainly. But no one doubted that the goal itself was part and parcel of Lincoln's persona.

What Lincoln offered the American people was not change for change's sake, but a moral commitment to the Union. And despite his lack of experience, Lincoln brought a maturity beyond his years. Self-educated, self-reliant, Lincoln possessed as deep an understanding of the nation's impending crisis as any man alive.

As for Obama, he's **selling change like some kind of hair-removal product.** *Ooh, change!* **Is Obama too young to realize that** *every* **election is about change?**

Has anyone told the young man that we change our President *every* four to eight years? Usually, the candidates are sufficiently experienced to know this stuff, and their platforms extend beyond just "change" to "the kind of change" they seek. Usually the candidates have been in the public arena long enough to understand how it all works.

Not so, Obama, apparently.

We still recall cringing when we heard Obama speak of his "experience" on the campaign trail. **At one point he was bragging about** *"what he majored in"* **back in college.** Isn't that the kind of thing a new graduate puts on a resume to fill up an otherwise empty page? That's certainly not the resume we expect from a candidate for the office of the President of the United States.

In this race, the second least-prepared candidate is facing the most prepared candidate of all time. Let's make a simple comparison: Your 16-year-old son with a fresh driver's license, vs. Richard Petty. Who are you going to put in the cockpit of a 200 mph race car? Or your 16-year-old daughter vs. Danica Patrick. Who is most likely to even finish the Indy 500? Exactly. Sit down, kids, and learn a thing or two from the experts.

Obama's handlers are doing their best to bulk up Obama's policy credentials, so that he can at least see over the top of the steering wheel and keep the car on the left—er, right side of the road.

There are daily attempts to show Obama as an athletic politician, capable of leaping the learning curves that would daunt a lesser man. Perhaps because his resume is so thin – he's the one-page candidate – he whips his intelligence out every chance he gets. He loves to talk to his audiences as if they were students. This habit became such a potential embarrassment for Obama late in his primary race that his advisors forbade him to use the "u" word. He had been starting every other sentence, it seemed, with the word "understand." Not as in, *"I understand the concerns you have."* More along the lines of, *"Understand that I'm smarter than you are."*

Well, let's see about that.

## Obama's gaffes could make Dan Quayle envious.

Quayle would be envious of how Obama's gaffes are ignored. When a conservative politician like Quayle makes a gaffe, the Leftstream Media hoists the dunce cap onto him for life. When a liberal politician makes a gaffe, the Leftstream Media excuses it for what it is—a mistake.

The campaign trail is brutal, not unlike the 24 hours of *Le Mans* only for 2,400 hours … driving, driving, driving … never resting. Every candidate, even the most able public speaker, makes verbal gaffes. Including Obama.

Columnist Michelle Malkin has called Obama *"a perpetual gaffe machine."* [51] Here are some of the gaffes that Malkin and other political analysts have tallied up.[52] If you look close enough at these slips of the tongue, you'll find all kinds of sinister and dark motives!

### *The 57 States of the Union*

Campaigning in Oregon, Obama said *"Over the last 15 months, we've traveled to every corner of the United States. I've now been in 57 states …"* Fifty-*seven* states? It's unfortunately true that many people don't know how many states we have—most of them vote Democratic. Is Obama one of them? Or was he playing to Democratic ignorance? Or was he confusing his countries? When this first happened, radio host Rush Limbaugh had a grand time pointing out that there are in fact 57 Islamic states. Was this a Muhammadan slip? Or was *Wall Street Journal* editor James Taranto correct when he noted that there are 50 U.S. States and seven Canadian provinces—so maybe Obama intends to sell the United States to Canada to raise money for all his spending programs.

## Afghan interpreters

Trying to showcase his foreign policy talents, Obama was blaming the Bush Administration for the shortage of interpreters in Afghanistan:

> We only have a certain number of them, and if they are all in Iraq, then it's harder for us to use them in Afghanistan.

Possibly. Or possibly it's because Iraqis speak Arabic and Kurdish, and Afghanis speak Pashto, Farsi and other non-Arabic languages. So we need different interpreters for each war.

## Tornados killing thousands!

> In case you missed it, this week there was a tragedy in Kansas. Ten thousand people died—an entire town destroyed.

Actual death toll: 12

## Location of Kentucky

Explaining why he was trailing Hillary in the Kentucky primary race, Obama said:

*Senator Clinton, I think, is much better known, coming from a nearby state of Arkansas. So it's not surprising that she would have an advantage in some of those states in the middle.*

Last we checked, Obama's "home" state of Illinois borders Kentucky, and Arkansas is a hike to the south. And, technically, Hillary hasn't lived in Arkansas for decades. But that's quibbling.

## Cold shoulder at the auto plant

Obama is fond of telling how he walked into the lion's den in Detroit, and he lectured those automakers to start making more fuel-efficient vehicles to protect our environment:

*When I delivered that speech, the room got really quiet. Nobody clapped.*

Actual video footage of the event shows the room far from quiet—Obama actually earned a hearty round of applause as well as a standing ovation. Is such truth-twisting part of the "new politics"?

## Hanford nuclear waste cleanup

Obama was asked about the nation's most contaminated nuclear waste site in Hanford, Washington, and had this to say:

*I'm not familiar with the Hanford site, so I don't know exactly what's going on there. Now, having said that, I promise you I'll learn about it by the time I leave here on the ride back to the airport.*

On the ride back to the airport, an aide probably told Obama that he voted at least once to spend billions to clean-up Hanford. A billion here, a billion there, pretty soon you ought to find out where it's all going. He did not understand his own vote.

## Life magazine fabrication

In his memoirs, Obama tells of seeing a copy of *Life* magazine at age nine, and in it were photos of a man physically and mentally scarred by his efforts to lighten his skin. Obama credits these photos with triggering his racial awakening. In fact, the photos never existed, according to *Life's* own historians. They were clever pigments—sorry, figments of a very active imagination.

## Obama's parents meeting in Selma

On the anniversary of the historic Bloody Sunday civil rights march in Selma, Obama told audiences:

> There was something stirring across the country because of what happened in Selma, Alabama, because some folks are willing to march across a bridge. So they got together and Barack Obama Jr. was born.

What a wonderful story! Except that Barack Jr. was born in 1961, four years before the Selma march. When asked to clarify, Obama's campaign said the candidate was *"speaking metaphorically about the civil rights movement as a whole."* Good, because we'd rather not hear any more personal details about liberal politicians and bridges.

## Threat of Iran

In Oregon, Obama told an audience that Iran does not *"pose a serious threat to us"* because *"tiny countries"* with small defense budgets can't hurt America. The very next day, looking a little roughed up from the verbal beating his handlers must have given him, Obama insisted, *"I've made it clear for years that the threat from Iran is grave."* Iran poses one of the greatest threats to world peace today—there is no disputing that. For the rookie Obama to botch such an important matter is seriously frightening.

## We're goners!

This one comes again from an Obama campaign stop in Oregon. Good thing liberals are busy hugging trees out there; they might be concerned about their man Obama. Especially after the science lesson he delivered:

> ...*China, India, in particular Brazil. They are growing so fast that they are consuming more and more energy and pretty soon, if their carbon footprint even approaches ours, we're goners.*

> Goners, I say!

> *We can't drive our SUVs and, you know, eat as much as we want and keep our homes on, you know, 72 degrees at all times.*[53]

Fortunately for Obama, his Oregon "goners" speech went unmentioned in *The New York Times, Chicago Tribune, Washington Post, Los Angeles Times, Associated Press, Reuters, NPR* and *NBC*. Wouldn't want to embarrass Obama.

## A man of the people

Trying to relate to folks in a small Iowa town, Obama sympathized, *"Anybody gone into Whole Foods lately and see what they charge for arugula?"*[54] You could hear crickets.

## *So many acronyms, so little time.*

Speaking in Orlando, Obama said he would meet with Venezuelan dictator Hugo Chávez to discuss Chávez's support of the violent Marxist FARC revolutionaries in Colombia. The next day, Obama was adamant that any country supporting the FARC should suffer *"regional isolation."* Did he flip-flop? Did he even know he contradicted himself?

## *Obstinacy is not policy.*

In a July 2007 debate Obama made the now famous pledge to *"meet, without precondition, the leaders of Iran, North Korea, Syria and Cuba."* He called President Bush's refusal to meet with them *"ridiculous."* When the criticism of his naiveté rolled in from all corners, rather than admit to the rookie blunder, Obama dug in.

He cited President Kennedy's 1961 summit with Soviet leader Khrushchev as a crucial step in ending the Cold War. In fact, Kennedy confided to advisers that Khrushchev *"beat the hell out of me."* The Soviet leader reported back to the Politburo that Kennedy was weak. Two months later, the Berlin Wall was erected. A year later Khrushchev shipped nuclear missiles to Cuba, and pointed them at the U.S. And for two decades we fought a Cold War until finally Ronald Reagan won it through a show of strength, not naiveté.

## Would Obama's resume be enough if he was white?

Talk radio host Michael Reagan hones in on the appeal of Obama:

> *He's the Halle Berry of American politics—he's a pretty, non-threatening face who happens to be the right color and, therefore, demands our plaudits. Never mind that he was brought up by his white mother, went to a*

*private high school and has spent about as much time facing down serious racism as Mitt Romney. He's got African genes, and we're all supposed to pull the lever for him to prove to ourselves that we're not racists.*

In other words, this election is about "race." It's not about Obama's resume. If a white guy ran for President with Obama's resume, he'd be a laughingstock. Check that. He wouldn't even be able to mount a campaign, and would never even come onto the national radar to be laughed at.

Dr. Martin Luther King Jr. fought against the hard bigotry of closed doors. He also fought the soft bigotry of low expectations. The first fight he won, the second not so much. Obama is proof of that among liberals. He had been praised as a once-in-a-generation leader, and for what? Surely not his accomplishments. So for what? His skin color? The fact that he's not Hillary? It's fair to say both are true.

Obama is a fine young man, period. When there's a little less green behind those ears of his, then he should look again at the presidency ... if over time he develops a coherent vision for our country that a majority of voters share.

For now, if Obama is elected President because we feel badly about a century of slavery, then we'll relearn the old maxim: If you want something badly, that's usually how you get it.

## Is Obama's patriotism heartfelt, or merely convenient?

Obama has wanted to be President since he was an island lad, to hear his friends tell it. Obama also appears to love this country, despite all the countersignals he sends. Such as showing up in public in October 2007 without an American flag lapel pin on his chest, when previously he had worn one.

Had he turned against his country? Or had he just forgot to wear the pin, which sounded more likely. These were odd questions to even be asking. Tempest in a teapot, and all that. But appearances do count, and symbols matter. So Obama was asked to explain:

> *Right after 9/11 I had a pin; that became a substitute for I think true patriotism, which is speaking out on issues that are of importance to our national security. I decided I won't wear that pin on my chest. Instead, I'm going to try to tell the American people what I believe will make this country great, and hopefully that will be a testament to my patriotism.*

It was a peculiar moment, and we initially dismissed it as evidence that Obama wasn't ready for prime time. Why would a relatively unknown Democrat seeking his party's nomination for President send such a sideways signal to voters? Why offend people unnecessarily? Where's the intelligence in that?

But we know Obama to be a bright guy.

Maybe he knew precisely what he was doing. He had already staked his candidacy on a U.S. military failure in Iraq. That war was going poorly, with public opinion turning against President Bush. He had a chance to double down on his anti-war bet. If the gamble paid off, he could leap ahead of Hillary in the primary contests still ahead. If he gambled wrong, he could run for President again in four or eight years. He was a young man, after all.

In retrospect, his instincts were brilliant.

The anti-war activists who run the Democratic Party went gaga over the lapel pin maneuver—deeming it a bold condemnation of the obviously-evil-corrupt-racist-babykillers currently in power. These liberal activists began deserting Hillary in droves, soon derailing her woman-power juggernaut. But gambling with fire has known consequences.

Six months after the lapel pin brouhaha, a controversy erupted over Obama's spiritual mentor. This story is well known, and we bring new revelations in Chapter 10 that speak to Obama's fitness for higher office. Right now, though, the story is about patriotism.

When Obama was forced to explain why he sat silently in a church pew for 20 years while his pastor spewed anti-America hatred, Obama took the stage and offered his explanation with a full complement of eight large American flags as his backdrop.

Having previously told us he was above patriotic symbolism, he quickly wrapped himself in patriotic symbolism when the heat was on. Edmund Burke once quipped that *"patriotism is the last refuge of scoundrels."* If Obama had a quip, it might well be: *"Patriotism – what the heck; let's give it a try."*

So is Obama's patriotism real, or merely convenient and possibly conflicted? Unless Obama clarifies his true feelings in the general campaign, voters may well conclude the worst.

## What Obama's "big" addiction reveals.

Little things can reveal the inner workings of the mind. Little things like smoking.

Obama smokes, like a cannon actually. His doctor says Obama has quit smoking *"on several occasions and is currently using Nicorette gum with success."*

Does Obama's nicotine addiction shock you, or offend you, or leave you somehow less willing to treat his candidacy charitably?

Obama fears voters will judge him harshly if they see him smoking. So on the campaign trail, he often devises clever ways to sneak a smoke when the press corps isn't looking. It can be quite entertaining watching his motorcade pull up behind the convenience mart, Obama dashing into the men's room, and a gaggle of reporters trying to follow him in.

Entertaining, if it wasn't such a ludicrous display.

Obama is at least half right in trying to hide his smoking habit. Many voters in California will definitely think less of him. Hashish, the hookah, fine. But cigarettes? Yuck! California liberals are so beyond all that. And nowhere in California are the politics more absolutely liberal than in San Francisco. Obama has lived his entire life with their kind, sipping espresso, freeing Tibet, blaming the morning fog on global warming which, as all of their friends know, was caused by George Bush and GOP dirty tricksters.

So when Obama's primary campaign was failing to gain any real traction in heartland states, Obama offered his bohemian San Francisco friends a rationalization:

> *You go into these small towns in Pennsylvania and, like a lot of small towns in the Midwest, the jobs have been gone now for 25 years and nothing's replaced them ... And they fell through the Clinton Administration, and the Bush Administration, and each successive administration has said that somehow these communities are gonna regenerate and they have not. And it's not surprising then they get bitter, they cling to guns or religion or antipathy to people who aren't like them or anti-immigrant sentiment or anti-trade sentiment as a way to explain their frustrations.*

The takeaway was *"bitter."* All of these middle-Americans are bitter losers in Obama's view, acting out their bitterness through such odd behavior as hunting and going to church. Bitter little people in forgettable little towns. And how does Obama know all this?

Well, because when he wasn't sneaking a smoke back in college, he was reading. Bitterness is something socialist professors understand. Bitterness, they write, is at the root of the American struggle. It is what drives the poor to rise up against the wealthy. It is the glorious dividend, and they invest their students as liberally as possible. A bright student like Obama would have devoured such master works as:

*Bitter Harvest: A History of California Farmworkers*

*Bitter Truth: Avant-Garde Art and the Great War*

*Bitter Fruit: the Story of the American Coup in Guatemala*

These kinds of books would now inform Obama's thinking in the same way that Ayn Rand and Friedrich von Hayek inform so many conservatives.

Obama is hoping that folks in the heartland will forget his little *faux pas* when he returns in the general campaign. But don't count on it. Obama will find it rather difficult to "connect" with folks who believe in traditional things, such as living in small towns where you know everybody, going to church most Sundays or otherwise gone hunting, believing that the less government in your life the better, flying a big American flag on the Fourth and plenty of other days, demanding that immigrants speak English and be here legally, and generally feeling that America is a fine country, thanks to folks like them.

Plain fact is, Obama knows nothing of middle-America—he has never felt their pain, or their joys. He has never known their world, nor even visited it outside of scheduled campaign stops. He hasn't even stopped to light up a cigarette with one of them, and shoot the breeze. (Instead, for his smokes, he sneaks around behind the gas station.) Through his actions he has revealed an underlying contempt for the heartland, and thus for the country itself. Sure, his speeches are full of pretty words about the promise of America, but his actions speak a different tune. It is a conflicted tune, made all the more discordant by the arrival at Obama's side of one man. This one man is heavily invested in Obama's success.

This man's twisted schemes, next.

# 8. Why A Secret Pact With The Mad Billionaire?

*It is a sort of disease when you consider yourself some kind of God, the creator of everything, but I feel comfortable about it now since I began to live it out.*

*Next to my fantasies about being God, I also have very strong fantasies of being mad...*

*America needs to follow the policies it has introduced in Germany ... we have to go through a certain de-Nazification process.*

*The main obstacle to a stable and just world order is the United States"* and we must *"puncture the bubble of American supremacy.*

*I am basically there to make money. I cannot and do not look at the social consequences of what I do.*

Would you stake your good name and reputation to someone who carries on like this? If you answered, "only at gunpoint," then you know how it feels to a Democratic Party leader today.

Yet even the most liberal Democrats try to shun the man born György Schwartz, who prefers to go by George Soros, and who has in fact said these loony things. Sure, Democrat candidates will take his money—nearly a half billion dollars will go from the Bank of Soros to pet left-wing causes this year. But every Democrat with a dram of dignity, or an alternative, publicly distances himself from Soros.

Everyone but Obama.[55]

# Every respectable liberal shunned Soros, except Obama.

Back in 2004, billionaire investor George Soros made a big splash when he purchased the Democratic Party lock, stock and daisy. It was a wildly embarrassing chapter in American politics, a chapter that continues into the 2008 election cycle, as we'll see.

But lost in the national spectacle of 2004 was a race in Illinois for an open seat in the U.S. Senate. A relatively unknown Illinois state lawmaker by the name of Barack Hussein Obama had bested a field of seven to become the Democratic nominee facing a wealthy, handsome Republican named Jack Ryan.

Obama was being outspent by an order of magnitude, and if he couldn't come up with a bundle of cash fast, his national political ambitions would die at the starting gate. Seemingly out of nowhere came Soros, dialing in with a radar for far-left causes. Soros hosted a fundraiser for Obama at his home, and raised enough cash to keep Obama's head above water for the short-run. Not only did Soros donate, but four other family members donated as well. In total, the Soros family gave $60,000 to Obama in that election.

Unexpectedly in the weeks afterward, Obama's opponent imploded as a candidate and Obama sailed through to victory. At his side, sharing in the victory and the spoils to come, was a beaming Soros.

Soros' own political agenda has long been to fill the campaign troughs for radically left and socialist politicians who, having eaten their fill like good little liberals, will hungrily respond to any Soros phone call that might promise even more money in the bank. Obama has proven himself an unrepentant Soros-fed pol.

Granted, the two men have been careful to be discrete over the years. They keep up appearances so as to not blatantly violate federal election laws which prohibit groups, like the many Soros controls, from intervening in a political campaign. But the relationship is solid.

Soros's goal in this race has been clear from the outset. He lost when he tried to buy the presidency in 2004. He's not planning to lose again. He desperately wants a President he can put up on the mantle. Just as he divorced his first wife as soon as he was wealthy enough to get a trophy wife, then divorced the second for an even younger hottie, he wants a trophy President. And he's using his vast resources to bring it about. To have "someone in the Oval" who will "take his calls" and treat him with the respect that has so far eluded him outside of the financial world.

Just as Obama showed no compunction about hopping into bed with, and seeking favors from Tony Rezko, the real estate developer who was under indictment at the time, Obama has been perfectly willing to be Soros's trophy President-to-be.

## Obama meets with Soros one last time, then announces.

In December 2006, Obama and Soros met in the latter's New York office one last time. What they discussed is unknown. But just one month later, Obama announced the creation of a Presidential exploratory committee. And within hours, Soros had contributed the maximum allowable $2,100 to Obama's campaign.

If 2004 is any indication, **Soros will spend 100,000 times as much as he is personally allowed by law to get Obama elected.** Some $200 million will be funneled through campaign finance law skirting groups to ensure a liberal victory. And if Soros determines that $200 million is simply not enough, he could easily spend double or triple that and never see a dent in his $7 billion bank account.

If Obama does become Soros' trophy President, what will the old man ask in return? The Democratic national leadership is so hungry for a win, they don't care what they hand over to Soros as long as the troughs runneth over with the kind of slop to which they've grown accustomed. They are frothing mad about losing twice to George Bush; their minds are bubbling over with revenge fantasies; they have so thoroughly convinced themselves that Republicans are evil, they can't remember ever thinking straight.

Despite whatever intelligence they may display in their normal lives, when it comes to politics Democrats have developed an almost pathological blindness to the most obvious of facts:

Both sides fight hard, and often. It's the same in politics as in business, in sports, and around the dinner table too often. People fight hard for what they want, and for what they believe in. That's what people do. But liberals are now so unhinged that they see themselves as the sole and righteous holders of the virtue torch. Is Obama as unhinged as the rest of them, as beholden to Soros and seemingly unstable as Howard "the screamer" Dean, Hillary "the whiner" Clinton, or John "reporting for duty" Kerry? Or is he cut from a different "new and improved' cloth, as his handlers insist?

To answer this question thoughtfully, we've look deeper into the relationship between Barack Obama and George Soros.

Much of their relationship has been conducted behind closed doors, with few leaks. This has given rise to intense speculation in the online blogs, and most of that speculation is baseless. But we are fortunate to know **well-placed currency traders who are privy to plans Soros has been hatching**. These sources have agreed, on condition of anonymity, to tell us all they know about the Soros-Obama nexus as it relates to the campaign ahead and the presidency beyond.

## Are Obama and Soros two burrs in a Donkey's tale?

As a Senator, Obama was the lead sponsor of the Global Poverty Act, the largest wealth redistribution project ever proposed. If passed, it will take $850 billion out of U.S. taxpayers' hands and put it into the hands of poor people overseas. That is Obama's hope, anyway.

Whose hands the poverty relief dollars will actually wind up in, is anybody's guess. First the United Nations will get a piece, and every corrupt bureaucrat at that shakedown organization will take their cut. Then, whatever's left will continue onto the world's most wretched poverty holes, almost all of which are run by brutal dictators and military juntas. These corrupt oppressors will then take their cut, feeding the troops that keep the people poor, using some of the food as bribes to keep local leaders in line.

Whatever scraps still remain will be tossed from the back of trucks into jostling crowds of starving children, with the media cameras dutifully relaying the images back home so that Obama and his liberal friends can feel good about the work they are doing. "Oh, those poor dears ... at least they're getting the best slop we could send ... pass me a little more arugula, won't you George?"

**For this global welfare boondoggle, Obama and his liberal friends in Congress are demanding that American taxpayers turn over hundreds of billions per year.**

And which official at the United Nations is in charge of this project? Leading the United Nations Millennium Project is a Columbia University professor named Jeffrey Sachs. In his 2005 book, *The End of Poverty,* Sachs wrote, *"Africa's governance is poor because Africa is poor."*

What?

This rather naïve, one-dimensional view of the world is what passes for intellectual rigor at Columbia.

When Soros read Sachs' book, he was naturally agog. He sought out Sachs and was so enthused about the brilliance of Sachs' Africa poverty solution, he convinced the good professor to head what would become the UN Millennium Project, with a $50 million grant from Soros to ensure its success, or at least its longevity. (That trough just gets bigger and bigger.)

Sachs began touring the world telling everyone that poverty could be eliminated in our lifetime if only U.S. taxpayers would dig deeper into their pockets.

On cue, Obama introduced legislation into the U.S. Senate to start the digging.

Were this but one example of Obama and Soros making one set of prints in the trail, it could be considered a fluke. But other prints can be found in Middle East politics.

Obama has made a big show of his support for Jewish concerns, a difficult task given his many past associations with anti-

Semites in the U.S. and abroad. As well, being a modern Democrat requires viewing the Israelis and Palestinians as equal partners in Mideast violence and failed peace initiatives.

**Soros is a Hungarian Jew who survived the Holocaust by pretending to be Aryan. He has said many loony things in his life and has admitted to being "quite rabid" in his political views. So when he accuses American Jews of fomenting anti-Semitism,[56] he should be ignored. But he's not. Not by Obama, anyway.**

One of Obama's long-time chief advisers is a fellow named Robert Malley. While working for Obama, Malley penned a number of articles together with an adviser to former PLO leader Yasser Arafat. These articles praised the community-building work of the Palestinian terrorist group Hamas, and directly blamed Israel for the collapse of the Israeli-Palestinian negotiations at Camp David in 2000. Malley's assertions have been denounced by everyone from President Clinton to the Republican leadership, as it was obvious to all participants and spectators alike that the peace talks failed when Arafat turned down an offer for a Palestinian state and instead launched a bloody intifada against the Jewish state.

When the Jewish media discovered that Malley was advising Obama on Mideast policy, the matzah hit the fan. Even the Leftstream Media joined in questioning Malley's views, so caustic and anti-Semitic were his views. Obama promptly fired Malley, who just as promptly went to work at the Soros-funded International Crisis Group, where he serves as Middle East and North Africa Program Director.[57] Malley will remain there, presumably, until such time that he might be able to go to work in an Obama State Department and, unfettered by the need to appease Jewish voters, resume his Israel-bashing, terrorist-hugging activities. We examine this further in Chapter 15.

# How Soros made Obama look like "a man of the people."

During the primary campaign, the "big story" on Obama was the grassroots support he was receiving from everyday Americans all across the country. And indeed, from 2007 forward Obama raised more than $100 million from Americans contributing $200 or less at a time, according to data compiled by the Campaign Finance Institute. This "little guy" theme remained in place until late in the Democratic primary when the party's deep pockets began shifting their big fat donations from Hillary to Obama.

Consequently, Obama looked every bit a man of the people. This pleased Soros considerably, for it was precisely the effect he had spent millions trying to convey. His polling showed that his trophy President-to-be was viewed across demographic groups as an inspiring populist leader with an everyman message. So powerful was that message that millions of people were scraping together whatever last few dollars they had and were sending those dollars to Obama!

If only it were true.

Our investigation of Federal Election Commission records on the contributions to Obama's campaign reveals that **Obama's contributors overlay almost in mirror image to the membership of MoveOn.org.** It's not a precise overlay because Obama has finally succeeded in mobilizing the black vote. But beyond the big bump Obama will receive from the 12% of America that is of African descent, the great bulk of Obama's support has come from MoveOn.org.

Basically, if you contributed to MoveOn.org over the last two elections in which they've been active, you gave to Obama in this election cycle. With 3.2 million active members, MoveOn.org has no equal in influencing elections. Their email outreach can mobilize a half million people in a day's time, flood an office with donations in an hour's time, and shut down a political opponent in a news cycle. They are the living, breathing heart and soul of today's Democratic Party. In fact, they own the party.

After raising more than $300 million for Democrats in 2004, **MoveOn.org director Eli Pariser declared:**

*Now it's our party. We bought it, we own it…*[58]

And who owns MoveOn.org? They have a nominal board of overseers, but they answer to one man—George Soros. He is their largest contributor and most influential arm twister. If Soros wants something, no matter how crazy, they make it happen for him. And they want to win this election badly. Together as a team, Soros and MoveOn.org lost the last two elections, despite spending $300 million. They don't plan to lose again. They know they've had some dog candidates to push in the past, but they believe they have an ideal situation this cycle—a disliked incumbent, a popular desire for change, and a fresh exciting candidate who has been positioned, artfully, as a man of the people.

Beholden to MoveOn.org.

**How many Americans, though, would approve of their Commander in Chief taking military policy direction from the same people who accuse our military generals of betraying their nation—the most grievous insult you can level at a career soldier?**

As chicanery goes, few episodes have been more despicable than MoveOn.org's attack ad against General David Petraeus, which ran in *The New York Times* in September 2007. This ad accused General Petraeus of "cooking the books for the White House," mocked him as "a military man constantly at war with the facts," and capped the verbal assault with the vicious taunt that he is "General Betray Us."

MoveOn.org is manning the barricades of a full-blown reincarnation of 1970s anti-war radicalism, only far better funded and not dragged down by all that distracting LSD and free love. General Petraeus is a fine man doing a difficult job he was ordered to do. As a soldier, he says *"Yes, sir!"* If anti-war activists want to attack George Bush for his military policies and strategies, have at it. Vigorously. But accusing a career soldier of "betrayal" is the lowest and most pernicious attack possible, wounding deeply.

We suspect MoveOn.org recognizes this, and chose to attack on a personal level to make the biggest media splash possible. They succeeded. All the more reason to question their having a seat at the grown-up table.

Every decent Democratic politician should have denounced that ad—immediately. Many did. It was so obviously beyond the pale. **What position did Obama take when his fellow Senators were rising up to denounce the ad?**

**Well, he missed that vote.**

**Continuing a long history of "being indisposed" when controversial votes come up.**

It's conceivable that Obama would have wanted to denounce that ad and MoveOn.org. But he couldn't risk upsetting Soros on something that was obviously so important to his benefactor: the attempt to humiliate a dedicated public servant. As Senator Lieberman has said:

> *This is the danger, that somebody who has real potential like Obama gets co-opted by people whose hostile view of America and how to protect it and advance it is so different from... the views of most Americans.*

## Inside sources tell of a Soros "October Surprise."

In politics, there is a rich history of October Surprises—big media events that whipsaw the momentum in a campaign just weeks or even days before voters go to the polls, creating a dramatic 5-10 point shift in polling numbers virtually overnight.

In 1968, President Johnson tried to help fellow Democrat Hubert Humphrey by announcing a wind-down of the Vietnam War (it failed).

In 1972, President Nixon's declaration that "peace is at hand" in Vietnam helped bury George McGovern.

In the 1980 election, there were charges that President Carter would finally rescue 52 U.S. hostages held for over a year by Iranian terrorists, and also that challenger Ronald Reagan had cut a secret side-deal with the Iranians to release the hostages after election day.

In 2000, candidate George Bush almost lost when, just days before the election, a Fox News reporter found that Bush had been arrested for drunk driving 24 years earlier (little came of this).

In 2004, Osama bin Laden released a threatening video just days before the election, possibly scaring some voters into sticking with the incumbent George Bush rather than an untested John Kerry.

These and other October Surprises are never sure things. They may work, they may be duds, they may backfire. But in a high-stakes election, they are part of the planning on both sides.

Soros knows that his views are radical, and unacceptable to most Americas. He knows voters can be fickle in the privacy of the voting booth. He knows his handpicked candidate is green. So he is definitely considering an October Surprise to thoroughly discredit the Republicans and sweep his candidate into the White House. He's willing to do *anything* to have influence again and to play out his mad delusion of *"being God."*

What kind of surprise?

Our sources tell us that Soros already knows how to trigger a devastating surprise. He has been working on it for more than a decade. And now, conveniently, the circumstances are ideal for his surprise. Best of all, in his eyes, it will combine his two great loves:

Making money, and picking Presidents.

Soros made his billions betting on the hard work of others. He never built anything, never created anything, he just gambled on the genius of others. And he did it well. He also managed to collapse the entire economy of England, and was found guilty of insider trading, stock manipulation, and trading fraud. But somewhere along the way, he decided that the capitalist world that had been so good to him shouldn't be so good for others. He wrote:

> *I am not so optimistic about capitalism ... it is built on false foundations...*

But not content to merely savage capitalism, he honed in on the true target of his discontent:

*The main obstacle to a stable and just world order is the United States ... we must puncture the bubble of American supremacy.*

That Soros is a hypocrite and loon is obvious. He admits to it himself. That he is capable of acting on his hypocrisy is equally obvious, and dangerous.

Soros has been shorting the U.S. dollar in global currency markets for several years, aggressively working to devalue the dollar. He has **helped devalue the dollar 30% in this decade alone**. (Note, the dollar would devalue with or without Soros help; U.S. government monetary policies are the major culprit here.) But this is serious damage done.

It is Soros' next steps that concern us.

**What would happen if Soros and highly-placed currency speculators all hit the currency markets in one coordinated strike?**

Nearly three trillion dollars a day trades on the world's currency exchanges. Ask any currency trader if it's possible for anyone to manipulate the currency markets given that much volume, and they'll laugh in your face. That's because they can't imagine anybody having a half-a-trillion dollars to play with.

Enter George Soros and a conspiracy of Asian and European currency traders, all hitting the currency markets on the same day, and crashing the dollar, sending Wall Street into a panic. The Dow could easily plunge 800 to 1,500 points as investors fear that the financial good times are finally over and the economy hopelessly lost. And who will be blamed for it all? President Bush and the Republicans.

If this scenario comes to pass, Obama is almost assured of a victory and the Democrats a clean sweep of Congress and a mandate to take government aggressively into the income redistribution business—*their collective end game.*

So what are the takeaways?

Obama has been launched from obscurity to within striking distance of the presidency largely as a result of one man's money. Obama might justifiably take offense at this statement, suggesting that his own talents have something to so with his stunningly swift rise to within grasp of the most important job in the world. But money is the mother's milk of politics. **Without Soros, Obama would probably be running for Mayor of Chicago.**

**Obama owes Soros, and that chit will be called**. And called. And called. What's more, Obama gives every indication that he will welcome the call. Obama's personal views aren't that different from Soros'. Obama is comfortable with a half-crazed socialist activist who is trying to end American supremacy and Republican rule by debasing the dollar, whose anti-American views resemble those of France, and who wants to see Israel knocked down to size.

It's rather startling to consider that the 2008 election could be decided by a megalomaniac who fancies himself some kind of God.

# 9. Couldn't The Media At Least Pretend To Be Fair?

**Leftstream Media bracing for "vast right wing conspiracy."**

Once upon a time in America, there was a rather harmless beast known as "Mainstream Media." This beast had taken an oath to report the news as fairly as possible. Like most fairy tales, there was enough truth to keep the fantasy alive. And across the land, all was well.

Alas, a terrible calamity drove the beast into hiding, never to be watched or read again. In its place arose an awkward new creature of clever tongue but stunted imagination. People gawked at this fledgling for years, not expecting it to survive—such were its limitations. But survive it did, and it became known as "Leftstream Media."

Nature abhors any imbalance in her news gathering world, so there was created the "Rightstream Media" to level the playing field – or at least equalize the population of gladiators in the news arena. Battle ensued. Leftstream held onto big-name newspapers and magazines, the cable news giant CNN, and the three TV networks. Rightstream made a play for talk radio, and took on CNN—besting both in audience sizes. But as the newer player to the news game, Rightstream operated at a disadvantage and often made the beginner mistake of trying to be "objective" in their reporting. Whenever it happened, you could practically see *The New York Times* building shaking from all the laughter within.

Each time audiences were measured through the 1980s, 1990s, and 2000s, the metrics edge belonged to the Leftstream. Nobody would dare admit it publicly, but the Leftstream has the edge in molding public opinion and swaying elections.

So we arrive at the 2008 election, and we find the Leftstream reporting a truly troubling turn of events. There is, they report, a vast right-wing conspiracy to lie, cheat, and smear their darling Obama. There is not, they report, a tough election being hotly contested on both sides. Absurd, they say.

Take the behavior of CNN's Wolf Blitzer. When the newsman snagged a big interview with Obama, he could have asked about Obama's strange friends, about his voting record, details of policy positions. But no, he asked if Obama was prepared for the "assault" from conservatives. How would they seek to smear him, Blitzer wanted to know.

Then there was *Newsweek* magazine running a 3,400-word cover story on how *"the Republican Party has been successfully scaring voters since 1968"* through some kind of secret *"innuendo and code."* Then there's the nagging question, non-existent until *Newsweek* raised it, of whether John McCain:

> ... can—or really wants to—rein in the merchants of slime and sellers of hate who populate the Internet and fund the 'independent expenditure' groups who exercise their freedom in ways that give a bad name to free speech.[59]

Was there a single word in either CNN's or *Newsweek's* big stories about the militant socialist attack machine that is expected to spend $1.5 billion defaming their opponents in this election?

No, not a word.

## Won't anybody put hard questions to Obama?

Once, late in the Democratic primary at a debate between Hillary and Obama, the sponsoring network ABC took a bold tact. They had their moderators Charles Gibson and George Stephanopoulos put genuinely difficult questions to Obama. Questions such as: why is Obama on social terms with radical Sixties terrorists who bombed U.S. landmarks and killed American citizens? Sounds like a fair enough question. But Obama erupted. It appeared to have been the first time in his adult life that anyone had asked him a hard question. He had been so accustomed to flattery and adulation from the media.

The second Obama scoffed at such an impudent question, that roar you heard was indignant editors in newsrooms across America rushing to their keyboards to proclaim their disgust at ABC's low tactics.

*Disgusting spectacle*
*(The New York Times)*

*Despicable ... slanted against Obama*
*(Washington Post)*

*Akin to a federal crime ... new benchmarks of degradation*
*(The New Yorker)*

*Disgraced democracy itself*
*(Philadelphia Daily News)*[60]

This nationwide outrage among the Leftstream Media continued for weeks. Editors talked of boycotts, and defamation hearings. It was a high and mighty tempest. All because a couple of reporters—Leftstream reporters, no less—had the audacity to ask a question of Obama that people would surely want an answer to.

If there is a queen bee in the liberal media hive, it is Maureen Dowd of *The New York Times*. She is known in liberal circles as a hard-hitting, hard-working journalist—an icon of credibility. To place that credibility in full view, she reported early in the campaign that Obama is an *"imperfect"* candidate as evidenced by the fact that *"his ears stick out."*

Upon hearing such brutal, stinging criticism, and then spying Ms. Dowd at a campaign rally, Obama marched up and scolded her:

*I just want to put you on notice. I'm very sensitive ... I was teased relentlessly when I was a kid about my big ears.*

To which Dowd replied, *"We're just trying to toughen you up."* The journalistic integrity and impartiality she showed here was truly inspiring!

Not one to pass on an open invitation, Rush Limbaugh went on air asking if this man *"lauded as the savior of the country, a Presidential candidate ready to be anointed, and he can't handle being teased about his big ears?"*

Limbaugh even nicknamed him "Barack Hussein Odumbo." All good fun. Of course Dowd and Obama were joshing. A small moment in all. But one that belied a larger concern—that the Leftstream Media see it as their duty to "toughen up" Obama. Not to report fairly his comings and goings. But to toughen him up.

**When they weren't toughening him up, the media was yanking him out of tight spots.**

When Obama got into trouble for telling hip San Francisco donors why people living in small towns "cling to guns and religion," the media invited him to clarify his meaning. As it was, he went right ahead and repeated the same basic ideas, only in slightly different words. He also expressed genuine surprise at the uproar he had caused—unable to even understand why he had offended so many people.

Recognizing the size of the hole Obama was digging himself into, the media leapt into action and began back-filling. They reported that Obama had cleared up the issue, it wasn't a big issue, there was no issue, move along please. Obama was spared any embarrassing apologies, thanks to his confederates in the media.

On another subject, drug abuse, the media took great pride in saying there was no reason to report Obama's teenage and college cocaine snorting because he had already "come clean" in his memoirs. They had the cover they needed to act as they intended. Does anyone for a second believe that if a Republican divulged his youthful drug habit, the media would lay off?

When the media had the chance to attack George Bush for cocaine snorting, they went at it with glee. They dug up an old widely-reported story, and acted like there were new revelations.

Or how about this? If a Republican were caught attending a concert featuring a rock band known to sing the Soviet national anthem, would they boil and chew on it for an entire news cycle?

Of course they would.

So why, when Obama folded a political rally into a concert with *The Decemberists* in Portland, did the Leftstream Media report not a peep of it? Says Robert Knight of the Media Research Center:

> *You'd think the media would find it interesting that a Presidential candidate had a band open for him that typically plays the Soviet national anthem, the song that celebrates communism in Russia ... but the media has taken no interest.*[61]

Obama knows the media will run cover for him while he grubs for votes among the disaffected, America-loathing youth of Portland.

# Obama's special place in the hearts of the Media.

Obama is everything the Leftstream Media could desire in a candidate. They enjoy a perfect alignment of political views; Obama's star power is a warm glow on reporters; the contest is legitimately historic; and the nation does yearn for a "change" from the policies of recent years.

## *Perfect Political Alignment*

Reporters who toil at *The New York Times*, *CNN* and the like are very different from ordinary Americans. That's a good thing. These reporters view themselves as smarter, more sophisticated, and just plain better than everyone else.

This superiority complex gives them a wide-ranging license to be arbitrary and contradictory in their reporting, without qualm. They are right, others are wrong, what's to question?

The righteousness of *The New York Times* was recently skewered in an exceedingly relevant way by Bernard Goldberg in *Crazies to the Left of Me, Wimps to the Right.*[62] Goldberg looked at *Times* coverage of the Iraq War and identified the true feelings and priorities of the *Times* and its readers, including Obama.

On one disheartening day in the Iraq War, two young American soldiers were brutally tortured and mutilated by terrorists in Baghdad, then paraded around for the attentive media. The *Times* dutifully gave the story page-one billing, once.

A few months earlier, the Abu Ghraib story had broke and the *Times* saw fit to run 61 page-one stories about how American soldiers abused Iraqi prisoners at that prison. Goldberg flayed the *Times*:

> *... this is not simply news coverage. It's a crusade. And no matter how honestly and objectively those stories were reported, together they amount to an editorial, masquerading as straight news. With Abu Ghraib, the Times found new angles to report every day. The paper ran stories on the accusations ... on the President's reaction ... on how an officer suggested the abuse was encouraged ... on command errors that aided the abuse ... on how an Iraqi recounted the abuse by U.S. soldiers ... on how the American guards at Abu Ghraib brought anguish to the unit's home in the United States ... on an American soldier who was a "picture of pride" but became a "symbol of abuse" ... on the connection between the abuses at Abu Ghraib and how "ill-prepared" and "overwhelmed" our soldiers are over there ... on the trials of the accused American soldiers, which were about to begin ... on the American head of*

> *the inquiry ... on an Afghan's account of U.S. abuse ...*
> *on prison policies that led to abuse on a whistleblower*
> *who "paints [a] scene of eager mayhem" ... on another jail*
> *that served as an "incubator for abuses in Iraq" ... on how*
> *the accused soldiers "try to shift blame in prison abuse" ...*
> *and on and on and on and on.*

As for the two young U.S. soldiers, the *Times* had nothing more except a small page eight sidebar many days later. These soldiers died fighting for their country; don't they deserve the respect of a few follow-up stories? Not from the *Times*. Their readers want to hear about the failings of Americans, not of terrorists. They have a point of view they bring to every war story: *"Terrorists are bad, but so are we."* Abu Ghraib is an example.

Obama has been an avid reader of the *Times* since attending one of the feeder schools for the *Times*, Columbia University. Does Obama agree with this slanted, hateful reporting that he reads in the *Times?* This is what he has said of Abu Ghraib:

> *...we know what the extremists say about us. America is*
> *just an occupying Army in Muslim lands, the shadow of*
> *a shrouded figure standing on a box at Abu Ghraib, the*
> *power behind the throne of a repressive leader.*

> *... in the dark halls of Abu Ghraib and the detention*
> *cells of Guantanamo, we have compromised our*
> *most precious values. What could have been a call*
> *to a generation has become an excuse for unchecked*
> *Presidential power. A tragedy that united us was turned*
> *into a political wedge issue used to divide us.*[63]

That Abu Ghraib was a disgraceful stain on the U.S. military, few will refute. Every war has its Abu Ghraib. It was an aberration—and should be treated so. In calling Abu Ghraib a political wedge issue, Obama is committing the sin he professes to abhor. He is not uniting, he is dividing. A genuine leader would put Abu Ghraib behind us by learning from it and acting on its lessons! It happened in 2004; this is 2008—why is Obama still focusing on it in the same anti-military way *The New York Times* focuses on it? To keep raising such a divisive issue at this point, tarring our soldiers and nation, makes Obama a typical reader of the *Times* but hardly a Commander in Chief.

## *Obama's Star Power*

Much has been made of Obama's charisma, the comparisons to Jack and Bobby Kennedy, the Reaganesque talent for lifting spirits. Obama's intelligence and personal magnetism are obvious to all. He brings genuine star power into the room. Nobody sees that more clearly than his friends in the media. Nearly everyone in the media sees something special in him. **Says former aide Julian Green:**

> *It's like nothing I've ever seen before ... we actually have fans among the media. I've never run across that for any other politician.*

With little coaxing from Obama's campaign, there began appearing headlines very early in the campaign, such as:

*"Dreaming of Obama"*

*"Great Expectations"*

*"Barack Obama Could Be The Next President"*

For reporters, it's a whole lot more fun hanging out with Obama than McCain. Obama's young and energetic, solid on both the basketball court and in the debating hall. But shouldn't Obama's political positions, and not his personal magnetism, drive the reporting we see about Obama in this campaign?

## *Historic Presidential Race*

Obama's success has many parents. First among them is the fact that Obama is an inspirational black leader who is *not* an obvious fraud. As *Chicago Tribune* columnist Clarence Page said of Obama's come-from-nowhere candidacy:

> *You know why? Because they finally got a black face for the party who's not Jesse Jackson or Al Sharpton. Let's be frank. That's how this thing got launched.*[64]

Most reporters, being liberals, get very uncomfortable asking questions about race. The whole subject makes them squirm. Oh sure, they are happy to talk about the "victims of white racism" and feel oh so virtuous about themselves. But they can't be honest and talk about the sticky issues, without first getting the nod of approval from black leaders. (A nod that isn't likely ever to come.)

So the hard questions, the ones that might lead to legitimate improvement in the lives of black people, don't get asked. As a public service to this campaign, we'll ask the questions:

**Mr. Obama, after all you've done for black Americans,** why do so many remain poor when millions of people of all races have moved up into the middle class? We agree that slavery was evil, and racism is terrible, but our nation as a whole is getting past that now. Why haven't some black people? It's been over 50 years since Rosa Parks refused to give up her seat on that bus. As a black leader, do you feel in any way responsible for this failure?

**Mr. Obama, after all you've done for black Americans,** why is the black illegitimacy rate today around 70% when it was around 20% in the 1950s, back when racism and prejudice was far more prevalent?

**Mr. Obama, after all you've done for black Americans,** a two part question: Why are 13-year old black girls bringing babies into this world; and why without any help from their black fathers?

**Mr. Obama, after all you've done for black Americans,** why do half of black inner-city kids drop out of high school?

**Mr. Obama, after all you've done for black Americans,** why do so many blacks wallow in Ebonics language that *ensures* that they'll never get a respectable job and escape poverty?

**Mr. Obama, are you going to use this historic campaign** to toss aside the empty bromides Democrats have fed blacks every since Martin Luther King Jr.? Are you going to come clean and admit that it is *not* racism that is keeping black Americans down? In short, are you going be honest?

These questions need asking. If anyone in the Leftstream Media has the guts to be honest and ask these questions, we welcome the company. But we're not holding our breath.

## *Genuine Desire for "Change"*

After eight years of an Administration headed by a Republican with some problems—reporters would embrace whomever came along. Obama is the beneficiary of this desperation.

In this sense, the media reflects the national mood. There is anger and frustration in America, most of it the result of the nation's collective credit card finally maxing out. Because people can no longer borrow against their house, or run up their credit any higher, they've turned sour. Compounding their ornery mood is a faraway war with a death toll that seems to be leading nowhere fast, a series of high-profile scandals on Wall Street and in Congress, a President spending taxpayer money like there's no tomorrow, and a vague sense that the American century is slipping away for good.

With all of this, America has understandably wished for a new face, a new direction, change of any kind. Nobody has wished harder than the media, and they possess the tools to make their wishes come true.

Tapping the power of these desires of the media—perfect political alignment, natural star power, a historic candidacy, and a desire for change—Obama's handlers have been able to catapult him in four short years from State Senator, to Bestselling Author, to United States Senator, to Chosen One.

## The Black Jesus, the Second Lincoln, the, the...

We wrote earlier of an art student in Chicago who sculpted an Obama-as-Jesus effigy. Turns out, many liberals are thinking the same thing. If you run a search on Google of "Obama + Jesus" you net about 783,000 hits! Sure, many of the entries are the blatherings of the blithering. But browsing the entries demonstrates very quickly the messianic appeal of Obama to ordinary Democrats. The candidate's appearances at rallies with his arms stretched to the heavens, while leading the gathered flock in ritual chants of *"Yes we can!"* certainly feeds the fervor. Obama *probably* doesn't think of himself as a prophet, but his admirers *definitely* do. And the media will offer all the hosannas that time allows.

For the more secular liberals, the far larger group, Obama's handlers turned to long-time liberal lion George McGovern to heap praise on Obama and compare him to Lincoln:

> *Illinois gave us Abraham Lincoln. That state may have now given us a second Abraham Lincoln.*

While the message may have inspired some, one wonders why the Obama campaign chose George McGovern to deliver it. Didn't he lose in a landslide to Richard Nixon?

Having lifted Obama up onto a pedestal, his supporters in the media are also insisting on setting the ground rules for the campaign. What's fair game and what's off-limits in this campaign? What are the rules the media will try to enforce? At various stops along the trail, Obama has issued his demands:

- Doesn't want to be called liberal (*"It's an unfair label, man!"*)

- Cannot question his national security credentials ("Cannot question something that doesn't exist!")

- Cannot talk about the huge welfare programs he has proposed ("Don't want to cause a race riot, do we?")

- Smarmy America-hating friends in Chicago get a pass ("They've served time, or are about to; haven't they suffered enough?")

- Everyone is to lay off his wife ("She didn't sign up for this hell!").

## Throwing the attack machine into overdrive.

The Leftstream Media is gearing up for the most offensive political offense our nation has ever seen. **The attack-dog politics employed by the Clinton's and Bushes have now been incorporated into the business plans of the media.**

They will attack with intensity, hurtling insult and invective at Republican candidates, making no differentiation between truth and fiction, flooding every medium with partisan shock and awe. Expect to see the media offering these images of Republican candidates:

- Attending Klan meetings

- Torturing helpless Muslim children

- Rebuilding World War II concentration camps

- Altering weather patterns

- Causing oil slicks

- Submerging populated islands

- Invading exotic new countries

- Drilling for oil in Yellowstone

- Clubbing baby harp seals

- Pushing little girls off of tricycles

And story after story will conclude, in ever more clever ways, that only an Obama victory can deliver us from all of this hell on earth.

When Obama gives his big acceptance speech at the convention, in Denver's Mile High Stadium, it will be on the night of the 45th anniversary of Dr. King's *"I Have A Dream"* speech and count on every breathless reporter to wax dreamy about Dr. King's vision finally becoming reality.

That this media barrage is more of a mirage will matter not in the least. That Republicans appointed the first black Supreme Court Justice, the first black Secretary of State, the first black female Secretary of State, the most diverse Cabinet in U.S. history, and helped usher the single greatest movement of black Americans into the middle class during Reagan's tenure, will go unmentioned.

Obama comes to this race with powerful allies. He also comes with some wildly embarrassing baggage from his days in Chicago.

# 10. Why All The Hate Spewing Friends?

*"The government ... wants us to sing 'God Bless America.' No, no, no, God damn America!"*

*"[America is the] No. 1 killer in the world"*

*"The government lied about inventing the HIV virus as a means of genocide against people of color."*

*"... what's going on in white America, U.S. of KKK A ..."*

*"The stuff we have done overseas is now brought right back to our own front yards. [9/11 means] America's chickens are coming home to roost."*

*"We bombed Hiroshima, we bombed Nagasaki, and we nuked far more than the thousands in New York and the Pentagon, and we never batted an eye"*

*"Racism is how this country was founded and how this country is still run!"*

*"We [in the U.S.] believe in white supremacy and black inferiority and believe it more than we believe in God."*

*"Louis Farrakhan is not my enemy. He did not put me in chains, he did not put me in slavery, and he didn't make me this color."*

*"Barack knows what it means living in a country and a culture that is controlled by rich white people. Hillary would never know that. Hillary ain't never been called a nigger. Hillary has never had a people defined as a non-person."*

*"Bill [Clinton] did us just like he did Monica Lewinsky; he was riding dirty" [said from the church pulpit while imitating a lewd sex act]*

*"The Israelis have illegally occupied Palestinian territories for over 40 years… the racism under which the Palestinians have lived because of Zionism."*

*"Fighting for peace is like raping for virginity."*

Again we must ask if you would even consider tying your fortunes to someone who talks this way?[65] And again you may reply "only at gunpoint." Not so, Obama.

He was proud to say that the author of these choice words, the Reverend Jeremiah Wright, was his surrogate father, a man he called "uncle," a man who married him, baptized his two daughters, and even provided the inspiration and title for his book detailing his vision for America.

Reverend Wright has received a thorough wash and rinse by the Rightstream Media, and a dye job by the Leftstream Media. But there are **new developments to this story**. We have also gained a deeper understanding of the complex relationship Obama had with Reverend Wright, and how it might impact an Obama presidency.

# The rest of the Reverend Wright story.

Hollywood producer David Geffen once said that *"all politicians lie; the Clinton's just do it with such ease."* If he weren't Obama's #1 supporter, Geffen might well say *'Obama plays the race card with such ease.'* And he's so good at it, we hardly notice. So how did he "play" the Reverend Wright story as it unfolded? Follow this timeline of events for a case study in using "race" to quiet white people into ignoring their better senses.

### March 2, 2008
### Hannity breaks the story.

Leading into Obama's Ides of March, Sean Hannity reports on *Fox News* of shocking developments in a church in Chicago, one that Obama himself has attended for the last twenty years. A guest on the show likens the church – Trinity United Church of Christ – to the deranged Branch Davidians of Texas.

### March 13, 2008
### *Leftstream media weigh in.*

After two weeks of hoping the story would die, but realizing it was a powder keg, ABC News broadcasts Reverend Wright's hateful vitriol into America's livingrooms. A shocked nation wonders if Obama's good friend and spiritual mentor of twenty years could really be such a racist crackpot who has on numerous occasions damned America, blamed the U.S. for 9/11, and accused the government of releasing the AIDS virus to keep down blacks. Disbelief reigns.

### March 14, 2008
### *Obama tries to hide the truth.*

When asked by reporters if these allegations could possibly be true, Obama deftly sidesteps the issue by claiming:

> *"None of [Wright's] statements were ones I had heard myself personally in the pews."*

### March 18, 2008
### *Obama delivers historic race speech.*

No longer able to sidestep the brewing controversy, Obama takes to the airwaves to deliver what is billed as an historic speech on race relations in America.

Having said four days earlier that he never heard Reverend Wright spew such hate, Obama now claims he was indeed sitting in the pews when his spiritual adviser carried on like a raving maniac. But in a clever head-fake, Obama takes the story in a different direction:

> *Not once in my conversations with [Wright] have I heard him talk about any ethnic group in derogatory terms.*

Obama wants us to differentiate between things the Reverend says in public, and things he says in private, as if this latter absolves him of any involvement whatsoever.

This is the first time in the campaign that Obama's mask slips off a bit, and voters can see that the "new face" of politics bears a rather striking resemblance to the old politics of, say, Hillary and Bill Clinton.

Early in Obama's race speech he plays the highest card in his hand, suggesting that white people should be ashamed of their reactions to Reverend Wright:

> *The fact that so many people are surprised to hear that anger in some of Reverend Wright's sermons simply reminds us of the old truism that the most segregated hour of American life occurs on Sunday morning.*

You can imagine liberals groaning under the weight of their guilt, for not knowing how neglectful they've been of the black churchgoing public. At this point Obama has burned through two outright lies and one guilt play. Next he ups the ante by sacrificing his own family honor:

> *I can no more disown [Wright] than I can my white grandmother—a woman who helped raise me, a woman who sacrificed again and again for me, a woman who loves me as much as she loves anything in this world, but a woman who once confessed her fear of black men who passed by her on the street, and who on more than one occasion has uttered racial or ethnic stereotypes that made me cringe.*

Makes us cringe, too. Cringe that Obama would drag his still-living grandmother's racism into public view for his personal gain. This is the woman who took him in and raised him when his own parents were off mainlining the free love movement and carrying water for communists. How could he stoop so low?

Desperation.

Obama knew his hand wasn't strong enough, he knew he was in trouble, and he was taking everyone down with him. In his frantic political calculus, Obama linked his grandmother's racism (however benign and long-ago) with his pastor's racism (however incendiary and current). Somehow, that was supposed to excuse both. But it didn't.

So Obama threw all of his cards on the table in one last desperate splurge:

> *I have asserted a firm conviction—a conviction rooted in my faith in God and my faith in the American people— that working together we can move beyond some of our old racial wounds, and that in fact we have no choice if we are to continue on the path of a more perfect union.*

Beautiful words certainly. But they failed to answer the big lingering question: If Obama cannot speak out plainly against the public bigotry of his spiritual mentor, how can he help move us beyond our so-called "racial wounds"? He can't.

## March 20, 2008
### Obama loses the "Typical White Grandmother" vote.

Public reaction to Obama's speech is generally positive, with media analysts suggesting that he played a bad hand expertly, and may even have emerged a stronger player. But still there are nagging questions such as: How could he credibly compare his white grandmother to the Reverend Wright? Obama, explains:

*The point I was making was not that my grandmother harbors any racial animosity. She doesn't. But she is a typical white person who, uh, if she sees somebody on the street that she doesn't know, there's a reaction that's been bred into our experiences that don't go away and that sometimes come out in the wrong way and that's just the nature of race in our society. We have to break through it.*

There's truth in this, and audacity as well. Here is a man trying to drag himself up out of a hole he spent twenty years digging, and he does it by referring to his grandmother as a *"typical white person."*

Imagine if John McCain had said such a thing! *The New York Times* would have pounced, labeling McCain a racist, bigot and ageist no doubt.

If Obama wants to present himself as the candidate of racial reconciliation, saying such dismissive things about little old white ladies is not the way to begin.

### *April 28, 2008*
### *Reverend Wright takes his show nationwide.*

Reverend Wright goes to the National Press Club and makes a spectacle of himself on national TV.[66] In a rambling Q&A session with reporters, Wright scolds them for airing his inflammatory remarks, saying it is:

*Not an attack on Jeremiah Wright, it is an attack on the black church.*

A reporter asks if Obama had regularly attended church and paid attention during sermons. Wright fires back:

*He goes to church about as much as you do. What did your pastor preach in the last week? You don't know!*

Elaborating on previous sermons demonizing the United States, the Reverend Wright holds firm to his teachings:

*You cannot do terrorism on other people and expect it never to come back on you. Those are biblical principles, not Jeremiah Wright bombastic, divisive principles.*

And on his 20 year relationship with Obama:

*Politicians say what they say and do what they do based on electability, based on sound bites, based on polls…*

And on his own ambitions, shared at a NAACP meeting, leaving a lot of people scratching their heads:

*Many in the corporate-owned media made it seem like I am running for the Oval Office. I am not running for the Oval Office.*

Will the Reverend Wright lead to Obama's undoing? The columnist Heather Robinson sees an eerie parallel to the aging Salieri in the movie *Amadeus*, who is driven mad with envy of the young Mozart:

*Seems to me Reverend Wright is the type who, unable to take pride in Obama's success or his own accomplishments … is actively working to undermine Obama. But Wright could not achieve this feat were Obama not genuinely tainted by this extremely dubious and very long-term connection.[67]*

### April 29, 2008
### *Obama finally denounces his spiritual advisor.*

Having said just ten days earlier that he could no more disown Reverend Wright than he could disown his church or his grandmother, Obama disowns Reverend Wright at a press conference in North Carolina:

*The insensitivity and the outrageousness of [Wright's] statements and his performance in the question and answer period yesterday I think shocked me; it surprised me ... they end up giving comfort to those who prey on hate ... they do not portray accurately the perspective of the black church ... They certainly don't portray accurately my values and beliefs. And if Reverend Wright thinks that that's political posturing, as he put it, then he doesn't know me very well. And based on his remarks yesterday, well, I might not know him as well as I thought.*

After all the two men have been through together, including Wright's being asked to lead the campaign's "African American Religious Leadership Committee," Obama then thrust the final knife:

*He was never my spiritual adviser.*

The facts of Obama's story shifted each time the spotlight intensified. Obama's mask began crumbling, and it was not a pretty sight. Thoughtful political commentators across the land began leveling unflattering assessments. From columnist Charles Krauthammer:

*It's hard to think of an act more blatantly expedient than renouncing Wright when his show, once done from the press club instead of the pulpit, could no longer be 'contextualized' as something whites could not understand and only Obama could explain in all its complexity. Turns out it was not that complex after all. Everyone understands it now. Even Obama.* [68]

By employing the Hillaryesque formula of only releasing a little truth at a time, Obama's entire credibility was called into question. Then in resorting to the race card and playing on white guilt, Obama went from being a candidate who happened to be black to the black candidate.

It's a shame how much damage Obama has inflicted on race relations in America.

# Why even join a church like Trinity?

Obama is free to worship where he pleases. Only when that choice of worship raises questions about the character of the man running for President is it appropriate to delve into the matter, going right back to his original reason for joining.

### *Identifying with the downtrodden.*

Obama has written of wanting to better understand how the downtrodden might achieve the equality promised in the Declaration of Independence. Having never felt hardship himself, he appeared doubly determined to feel it in the struggles of others:

> ... the struggles of Martin and Malcolm and unheralded marchers ... the voices of Japanese families interned behind barbed wire; young Russian Jews ... in Lower East Side sweatshops; dust-bowl farmers loading up their trucks with the remains of shattered lives ... I hear all of these voices clamoring for recognition.

In Reverend Wright's church, Obama found these clamoring voices and they filled an empty voice deep within. In the Reverend Wright's radically socialist weekly rants, and in the regular references to Marxist dogma, Obama found comfort and common cause.

### *Needing Farrakhan's blessing.*

For decades the route to political office in the South Chicago precincts has run through the offices of Nation of Islam leader Louis Farrakhan. His power has been unchallenged. An obligatory kissing of his ring was not enough to obtain his blessing. An aspiring black leader had to pledge his allegiance to Farrakhan's agenda of hate.

One could certainly hope that Obama, with his fancy education and new generation politics, could have avoided such an unsavory connection to Farrakhan. Didn't happen.

Obama moved into a mansion just down the street from Farrakhan's. They would be seen together from time to time at Muslim gatherings. When the Reverend Wright traveled to Libya with Farrakhan to meet with the international terrorist Muammar Gaddafi, and then bestowed a lifetime achievement award on Farrakhan, Obama was there applauding. He had found *"his people."*

### Believing in "Black Liberation Theology."

Of all the churches in South Chicago, Obama chose the one *known* to have a "Black Value System." At Trinity United, the word "black" is both adjective and noun. It is used to assert not only a racial difference, but racial superiority.

At the very heart of Trinity United were some wildly radical teachings known as "Black Liberation Theology." Most whites have never heard of it, by design. In these teachings, there is a God who commands people to rise up and demand that government: (1) create subsidized jobs for them, (2) guarantee healthcare and education by putting government in control of both, (3) achieve economic equality by redistributing wealth through massive taxes on the affluent and generous entitlements for the poor.

It is this blacks-first socialism that Reverend Wright preached from the pulpit while Obama looked up, listening. As described by its founder, James Cone of New York's Union Theological Seminary, Black Liberation Theology hails a God who sends whites to the back of the bus:

> *Black theology refuses to accept a God who is not identified totally with the goals of the black community. If God is not for us and against white people, then he is a murderer, and we had better kill him. The task of black theology is to kill Gods who do not belong to the*

*black community. . . . Black theology will accept only
the love of God which participates in the destruction
of the white enemy. What we need is the divine love as
expressed in Black Power, which is the power of black
people to destroy their oppressors here and now by any
means at their disposal. Unless God is participating in
this holy activity, we must reject his love.[69]*

You could be forgiven for thinking we're making this stuff
up. Sadly, no such luck. One need only visit Trinity United's
website and read the angry entries from the pastor's pen. It's all
there.[70]

Just as Obama was all there, soaking in this racist disgusting
drivel, for twenty long years. Did it have any effect on him? How
couldn't it?

His campaign speeches suggest a man determined to leave
his past behind him as fast as possible. But it's never so easy, even
if the desire *is* there.

**Can Obama just walk away and pretend he wasn't
jumping up and down in the aisle with Michelle and the other
parishioners when the "kill whitey" sermons and the "destroy
the white oppressors" chants were shaking the floorboards of
Trinity United?**

**Can Obama just walk away from twenty years of the Rever-
end Wright's "mentoring", such as when Wright has insisted that
the "black culture is more criminal," and that, well, it's simply a
travesty how blacks who "never got caught" treat blacks "who are
incarcerated" with disrespect?[71]** Wonder where Wright get this
drivel? In this case, the ideas are from University of Pennsylvania
law professor, Regina Austin. Black brothers and sisters, Austin
argues, should embrace the criminals in their midst as a form of
resistance to white oppression. They should become *"good hus-
tlers"* to create a *"middle ground between straightness and more extreme forms of lawbreaking."* As for examples of lawlessness, Austin
provides plenty:

Clerks in stores can cut their friends a break on merchandise. Pilfering employees can generously spread their contraband around the neighborhood.

That these proposals are silly and Professor Austin ought to have her home broken into a few times just for kicks, is plenty obvious. That she should be kicked out of academia and be forced to pay for the education she surely got free with affirmative action, is also obvious. Not so clear is (1) how a pastor like Reverend Wright could recommend this kook's code of conduct to the congregation week after week, and (2) how Obama could sponge it up and not have it color his own world view.

**Can Obama just walk away from his pastor's unequivocal demands that Ebonics be incorporated into the curriculum of all our public schools—to "validate the black experience"?**[72] Yes, even Ebonics! The Reverend Wright has praised the work of Geneva Smitherman of Michigan State University, who is leading the Ebonics charge. It's all so absurd. It strains credulity. And yet, somehow, it is true.

Black superiority, a black-only God, sanctioned crime, Ebonics in schools—are these the ideas of Obama or Obama's closest advisors, and will they be carried into the White House? That's the logical conclusion. And what else can we expect?

Based on the radical motley crew Obama has associated with to date, we wouldn't be surprised if one of Obama's crazy "uncles" took over a new cabinet level agency in charge of paying reparations to the families of slaves. Again, that's the logical conclusion.

The raw unvarnished fact is: **If Obama showed up in church even half the time over the last twenty years, he spent some 1,600 hours soaking in hate-filled, anti-American black nationalism.** Not once in all those hours did he stand up and challenge a radical ideology that would have shocked even his own open-minded mother. Not once has he since expressed any remorse at having subjected his two young daughters for their entire lives to this anti-white vitriol.

What could he have been thinking?

Or *was* he thinking?  Was he driven by a visceral insecurity, a gut need to seen as **a black man** and not a Caucasian/black man?

Perhaps.

It would certainly explain his near complete disavowal of the values of his white grandparents.

## In joining Trinity, he rejected his upbringing.

It wasn't Trinity United's black value system that raised and nurtured Obama.  It's wasn't an Afrocentric learning style, or a thumbing of whitey.  Obama's white mother labored hard, as Obama himself explains, to give him a well-rounded liberal arts education.  Obama's white grandparents raised him on prairie home virtues, a protestant work ethic, and white family values.  There wasn't any racial hatred in his upbringing.  By all accounts, that was his great fortune. Obama's ability to step into the American mainstream and to succeed was a result of uniting with whites, not damning them.

So how did Obama reconcile this obvious contradiction?  Shelby Steele, a mulatto himself, has written extensively and beautifully about Obama's upbringing.  In Steele's view:

> *Obama is also the kind of man who can close down the best part of himself to belong to this black church and, more broadly, to the black identity. This is the sort of habit that, over time, can leave a person without much of a self...*[73]

## At one point, why not just walk out?

Everyone pulls "boneheaded" stunts, as Obama likes to call his mistakes, from time to time. But our mistakes are supposed to make us stronger, sharpen our judgment, build character and all that.  In sticking with Trinity United for so long, has Obama shown himself to be weak, lacking in judgment, or deficient in character?

A thousand explanations have been offered for his refusal to walk out of that church. All of these explanations seem somehow insufficient.

## Did Obama desperately need a father figure?

In his memoirs, Obama tells how the good Reverend was there for him when his own father had never been. In *Dreams From My Father* the reader is struck by how naïve and impressionable young Obama was, and how he was clearly caught in a fierce internal struggle with identity issues, made sharper by the absence of a father. One can feel sorry for him in this regard. But the consolation prize is not the presidency.

In this view, Obama held onto Reverend Wright's dashiki out of love, and loyalty. But we think Obama is too smart to ride loyalty over a cliff. There must be another explanation.

## Was Obama energized by fanatic hatred?

Those who are predisposed to disliking Obama for extremely partisan reasons will insist that Obama actually enjoyed dipping into the hate pool on Sunday mornings. Just as kids eat up horror movies, Obama devours hate. And Obama did name his book *The Audacity of Hope* after one of the first sermons he heard Reverend Wright deliver. Obama quoted some of Reverend Wright's more outlandish opinions in the book. Obama participated in Trinity United functions that sought to break with white "middleclassness." And Obama soaked in Reverend Wright's wacky comparison of the brutal Sharpeville massacre of 69 blacks in South Africa to the U.S. dropping the atom bomb on Hiroshima. So it is not hard to conclude that Obama gets some kind of perverse thrill from trafficking in hate.

We think there is another explanation.

## Did Obama just sleep through it all?

It has been suggested, with some seriousness, that Obama went to church on Sunday to meet and greet the 8,000 potential voters in the congregation, but his interest in the preacher's blatherings was limited. The female columnist Star Parker has written:

*Religion for Senator Obama is not something too serious. It may satisfy some social needs and provide intellectual and emotional salve. But it doesn't translate into behavioral absolutes. The arena for addressing life's dilemmas for Obama is politics not religion.*[74]

Taking the point a step further from more of a male perspective is Michael Reagan:

*... you need to understand the way husbands and wives practice their religion these days. The men in the pews for the most part are passive, while the wives tend to be passionate. In most cases husbands are there because their wives have dragged them there. Chances are that while the women sit in rapt attention to the words of their pastor, the husbands are snoozing, blissfully unaware of what the reverend is preaching ... From what we've heard from Mrs. Obama, she was paying close attention ... as Barack dozed beside her, wondering when the Reverend Wright was going to shut up.*[75]

We find these explanations compelling, and they are buttressed by Obama's own writings on religion. As noted earlier, Obama's religious views more closely resembled those of his mother's:

*For my mother, organized religion too often dressed up closed-mindedness in the garb of piety, cruelty and oppression in the cloak of righteousness ... Religion was an expression of human culture, she would explain, not its wellspring, just one of the many ways—and not necessarily the best way—that man attempted to control the unknowable and understand the deeper truths about our lives.*[76]

Taking Obama at his word, and recognizing the breakneck schedule he kept for so many years (*"What better time to sleep than in church,"* you can imagine him admitting to pals), it's entirely possible that Obama was entirely tuned out while his pastor ranted in the pulpit.

If so, if Obama did in fact spend twenty years as an intimate of the Reverend Wright without ever having an inkling that the guy is a wacko hatemonger, then put a fork in Obama. We can't think of anything more terrifying than sending sleepy boy to the White House.

But we don't think this explanation quite hits home either. There may still be another explanation.

## Was Obama afraid to offend black people?

The black Philadelphia preacher, Derick Wilson, has written in the *Philadelphia Daily News* that Obama is a *"house Negro"* for not supporting Wright.[77]

Wilson could be written off as a crackpot, but there are others, many others, saying and writing similar things. *Chicago Sun-Times* columnist Mary Mitchell details the problem Obama faced in denouncing his pastor and church:[78]

> *This is a sad day for Black America ... when Obama says he is 'offended' by Wright's latest comments ... he's opening up a can of worms ... there is no institution in the black community more respected than the black church. And the notion that white pundits can dictate what constitutes unacceptable speech in the black church is repulsive to most black people.*

So Obama was stuck. He couldn't simply "change" church-es without offending a big swath of the black community whose votes he depended on. To that community, the Reverend Wright is black. Black is always right. White is always wrong. The color of one's skin trumps the content of their character. This daft race-centered world view differs little from the old white supremacy, but it is the world view Obama chose for himself.

So, is the reason Obama didn't walk out of Trinity that he was stuck? Perhaps, but we think it's more complex. **We think Trinity will ultimately be viewed as Obama's unexplainable "fatal flaw."** With the Clintons we were treated to daily case studies in fatal flaws. We were constantly amazed at how a seem-ingly intelligent, capable man could time and again hoist himself in his own petard.

Create a thundering embarrassment. Lie about it. Get caught. Try to wiggle free. Lie some more. Deeply wound peo-ple close to you. Beg forgiveness. Blunder again. Lie about it…

We recognize the Clinton pattern all too well, now. Does this moral bankruptcy apply to Obama as well? If it does, better to recognize it, and extinguish it, **before we're stuck with it**.

# Any other crazy (terrorist) uncles in Obama's attic?

On strident conservative websites, there is plenty of chatter about Obama's terrorist sympathies. Some wonder if Obama is a Manchurian candidate, or the smooth face of some sleeper cell waiting for the go-code from bin Laden himself. Others detail the elaborate 30-year campaign by Islamofascists to undermine the U.S. government, and wonder if Obama has been groomed from his birth as a Muslim as a one-day agent of destruction. Our intent here is to detail the things we know, and leave the speculation to others.

Obama's long friendship with the Reverend Wright has raised legitimate questions, potentially compromising Obama's candidacy though not condemning Obama's candidacy. That

131

doesn't begin until we meet the rest of the skeletons known to be rousting about Obama's attic.

When Obama chose the Chicago neighborhood of Hyde Park as his home, he sent an unmistakable message of who he was. Hyde Park is considered an oasis of coexistence—excruciatingly biracial, fiercely intellectual, and militantly socialist. Some have called Hyde Park and the neighboring University of Chicago, the Home of Humorless Liberalism, though Harvard and Berkeley would gallantly dispute that.

**This is home to the Democratic Socialists of America (DSA). This is their power base.**

**Obama knew all of this when he first arrived** in his old beat-up Honda Civic to work among the people. Obama's new employers and co-workers were all proud members of DSA, eager to enlighten this bright young man with their utopian visions. Like everyone else in the neighborhood, Obama welcomed the DSA into his life. He felt as one with them.

So when Obama ran for the Illinois Senate, he **proudly accepted DSA's endorsement**, and kept close relations through his Illinois Senate years and into the U.S. Senate. So close that when openly socialist Bernie Sanders ran for Senator in Vermont, Obama traveled there to urge voters to send Sanders to Washington to *"stir up some trouble."* [79] In return, Sanders called Obama *"one of the great leaders of the United States Senate,"* even though Obama had only been in the Senate for two years at the time.

When Obama announced for President, his list of socialist backers grew in numbers and enthusiasm. One of his endorsers is Rep. Jan Schakowsky, famous for being married to Robert Creamer who did time for using his liberal nonprofit group to shakedown businesses—in the tradition of Capone and Daley. In prison, Creamer penned a book on the future of Democratic politics:

> *Some people think that in order to win, Democrats need to move to the political center by adopting conservative values and splitting the difference between progressive and conservative positions. History shows they are*

*wrong. To win the next election and to win in the long term, we need to redefine the political center.*[80]

In other words, Creamer and Obama feel the need to transform traditional centrism into leftism. After his release from prison, Obama's good friend Creamer went to work for George Soros at the Open Society Policy Center—a holding tank for felons and socialist fanatics hoping to snap-up senior positions in an Obama Administration.

Clearly Obama hasn't just been breaking bread with socialists; he has been carrying their water for over twenty years. If Obama is a true socialist at heart, that's his business. But if he runs for President acting like some moderate, it's our business to look into it.

## Sipping espressos with anti-Semites.

For an Arab-American scholar to make the pages of the *National Enquirer*, quite a controversy must be generated. University of Chicago professor Rashid Khalidi accomplished this feat with an article titled "Obama's Secrets." In it, he blasted Israel. The professor's anti-Semitic flamboyance was no surprise to those familiar with Khalidi's work on behalf of the Palestine Liberation Organization at a time when it was correctly labeled by the State Department as a terrorist group.[81]

With credentials like these, Khalidi would naturally gravitate to Obama. He joined Obama in his 2000 campaign for Senate. Fellow campaign staffers have reported that **Khalidi was obsessed with an Obama victory**.

Khalidi also paved the way for Obama to join him as a member of the board of the Woods Fund. This foundation is active in radical Chicago politics, funneling money to a number of groups such as the Arab American Action Network. Outwardly, this network purports to be a social service agency. But its private activities have never been fully understood.

In his U.S. Senate race, Obama responded to questions emailed to him from the *Chicago Jewish News*. In his responses, Obama denounced Israel's fence, calling it a "barrier to peace" and he said the U.S. should work with Arafat—even though Arafat's missiles and suicide bombers were raining down on Israel at that period in time.

When Obama's responses became public, Jews and many Christians were outraged. Obama stepped into the breach and claimed that there was a terrible confusion; the responses were in fact not his; a low-level intern had mistakenly supplied them. (This would become a stock alibi of Obama's.) In this instance, Obama appeared to be lying. We learned this when Obama's Policy Director, Audra Wilson, told political commentator Debbie Schlussel that *she* had supplied the responses and in conversations with her boss, he had blamed the Mideast conflict on the Jews.[82]

Then there is Obama's long-time friendship with Palestinian activist Ali Abunimah. Obama shared the lead table at a fundraiser for Abunimah in 1998 with the late Edward Said, a prominent adviser to Arafat. Among Arabs, Obama's views were apparently clear. He blamed Israel for the lack of peace in the Mideast. But as he became more interested in obtaining Jewish donors and votes, according to Abunimah, he softened his views. When the two met more recently Obama told his old Arab pal:

> *I'm sorry I haven't said more about Palestine right now, but we are in a tough primary race. I'm hoping when things calm down I can be more up front.*[83]

Was Obama being honest with his friend Abunimah, or brushing him off? As we are known by the company we keep, Debbie Schlussel has done some looking into the company Obama keeps, cultivating inside sources for information.

One source has suggested that a close eye be kept on Bettylu Saltzman. She *"has Obama's ear on the Mideast and 'will be a major policy person' for Barack."* A major donor to Obama's campaign, Saltzman is also an officer of a trash-Israel group, and she has praised Jimmy Carter for calling Israel an apartheid state. This is only one source, and thus potentially unreliable. But the information is consistent with Obama's anti-Israel policy positions dating to his early Chicago lawmaker days, back before his was obligated to court Jewish donors, back before he realized how painfully embarrassing this friendships would become.

## Forced to publicly denounce old friend Farrakhan.

When Louis Farrakhan publicly endorsed Obama at a Nation of Islam conference in Chicago, NBC News reporter and host of *Meet the Press*, the late Tim Russert, asked Obama if he was happy to accept the endorsement of a man who called Judaism *"gutter religion."*

Obama replied, *"I can't say to somebody that he can't say that he thinks I'm a good guy."* With that, Obama broke out in laughter. There are times to laugh, and times to stifle the giggles. One example of that is when your political fortunes are being tied to the biggest name in Islamic rage and anti-Semitism. The blank expression on Russert's face probably snapped Obama out of his smug reverie. For he then promptly denounced Farrakhan—even though the Nation of Islam leader had just pressed his radical network of mosques into service for Obama's campaign.

Since Farrakhan has enjoyed a long history with Obama's church, Obama's sudden denunciation of Farrakhan did little to quell the mounting suspicion that radical Arabs held sway over Obama. So once again, this time at a townhall meeting in Pennsylvania, Obama tried to distance himself from Farrakhan's hateful message:

> I've been very clear in saying that that's wrong... nobody has spoken out more fiercely on the issue of anti-Semitism than I have.[84]

His answer was enough for his adoring fans. But for any genuine friend of Israel, it remained suspect. Especially since

**Obama continues to employ Farrakhan's people in high-level positions** in his Senate office and campaign.[85]

Nation of Islam's Shakir Muhammad handled campaign duties for Obama when he ran for Illinois State Senate. Nation of Islam's Cynthia Miller was treasurer of his U.S. Senate campaign. Nation of Islam's Jennifer Mason is Director of Constituent Services in his Senate office. Obama hasn't seen any problem with these people holding important jobs in his offices—despite their public devotion to the radical Nation of Islam credo. So Obama's condemnation of Farrakhan rings rather hollow. And it begs the question:

How many Nation of Islam hatemongers would find their way into senior positions in an Obama White House?

## Cavorting with groovy terrorists.

In the long stretch of Democratic primary contests, there were so many debates devoid of substance that even the Leftstream Media grew weary of showing up. So in one debate, the moderator George Stephanopoulos ignored the furor that was sure to be caused, and asked Obama about his friendship with William Ayers and Bernadine Dohrn.

"Bill and Bern" live down the street from Obama. They are quite the fixture in rad-chic Chicago politics. They've held a number of campaign functions for Obama at their house. Oh, and they personally carried out 25 bombings of U.S. landmarks as leaders of the Weather Underground in the 1970s, killed innocent bystanders and caused tremendous destruction. They went on the lam until a rich Daddy pulled some strings, and remain coldly unrepentant today. So, Stephanopoulos wanted to know, was this a problem for Obama?

It was the first time Obama had been asked to answer a difficult question, and he exploded in barely contained anger. He then gave his media questioner a tongue-lashing:

*This is an example of what I've been talking about. This is a guy who lives in my neighborhood, who's a professor of English in Chicago who I know and who I have not received some official endorsement from. He's not somebody who I exchange ideas from on a regular basis. And the notion that somehow as a consequence of me knowing somebody who engaged in detestable acts 40 years ago, when I was 8 years old, somehow reflects on me and my values doesn't make much sense ... so this kind of game in which anybody who I know, regardless of how flimsy the relationship is, that somehow their ideas could be attributed to me, I think the American people are smarter than that.*

Are we smarter than that? Well, let's see just *"how flimsy the relationship"* is between these Chicago neighbors.

- Twenty years ago the Chicago law firm of Sidley Austin hired Barack Obama, Michelle Obama, and Bernadine Dohrn. Though not all hired at the same time, they did work together and become friends and, obviously, lovers.

- When Obama ran for state Senate in 1995, his first campaign event was at the home of Bill and Bern. It was by all accounts quite the smash since the hosts are known locally as the "Bonnie and Clyde of the Sixties" and on everyone's party A-list.

- In 1997, Obama quoted Bill Ayers contributions to the field of criminal justice in a *Chicago Tribune* article. What contribution? That if your daddy's rich you won't do time? Is that the kind of legal precedent Obama should be citing? Does it say anything about the closeness of the two men?

- Coincidentally, on September 11, 2001 Bill Ayers gave an interview to *The New York Times* in which he said *"I don't regret setting bombs; I feel we didn't do enough."* At the time, Ayres and Obama were both members of the board of the prominent Chicago Woods Fund—and communicating regularly about the Fund's social agenda.

- In 2001, Bill Ayers made clear his continuing contempt for America by posing for a cover photo for a Chicago magazine. In the photo, he stomped all over an American flag. At the same time, Ayers made a $200 contribution to Obama's campaign.

Is this a flimsy connection? It appears quite the opposite to us—strong and enduring with meaning. But in fact there's more as related by the website Buck Naked Politics:

> *In 1995, the Chicago Annenberg Challenge was created to raise funds to help reform the Chicago public schools. One of the architects of the Challenge was none other than Professor Bill Ayers. Ayers co-wrote the initial grant proposal … And who did [Ayers] select as the new director of the board for this program? Barack Obama. Barack Obama was the first Chairman of the Board of the Chicago Annenberg Challenge … essentially an employee of Bill Ayers for eight years.*[86]

Taking this long connection a step further is columnist Mary Grabar who has dug into the blood and guts of Chicago politics, where the opening question in any transaction is: *"Who sent you?"* Because as the saying goes, *"We don't want nobody that nobody sent."* It's the modern Democratic machine in action, only slightly gussied-up from the original gangster version.[87]

So when, after only two years at Harvard and not yet head of the Law Review, Obama came looking for a job at swank left wing law firm Sidley Austin, he would not have been given the time of day unless someone had "sent him." Who could that have been?

A few years before, Obama had worked for Bill Ayres. Bill's dad ran Commonwealth Edison and that company's law firm was Sidley Austin. With one call, the red carpet would roll out for Obama.

There was no wrongdoing, as far as we know. Obama was simply networking his way up into Chicago politics proper. But when Obama later pretended in the debate to barely know Ayres, inquisitive minds became very eager to know what he might be hiding.

It's more likely that Obama knew his twenty year relationship to Bill Ayres, like his twenty year relationship with Trinity United, would become as toxic and damaging to his campaign as say, dynamite and murder.

**Nobody would suggest that Obama somehow endorses the bombings of the Pentagon, the U.S. Capitol and other buildings that his friends carried out. But neither can anyone of conscience fathom how Obama could maintain such a long friendship with their ilk.**

No candidate for office will have a squeaky clean list of friends and associates. That's not a fair litmus test. But when that list is far from clean, with many unsavory characters past and present, it matters. For the truest measure of a man is his choice of friends with whom he can proudly stand shoulder to shoulder, and not be forced to apologize.

When that measure is found wanting, then it is natural to begin questioning other things about the man…

## Why doesn't Obama cover his heart during the national anthem?

Refusing to wear an American flag lapel pin he had previously worn. Refusing to show reverence to a flag he had previously revered. These kinds of stunts may whip up the anti-America radicals who helped propel Obama from obscurity to national prominence practically overnight. But when a candidate for President is happy to be photographed turning his back on the flag and slouching, then Americans can feel happy turning their back on his candidacy and leaning toward someone who is clearly proud of the Stars and Stripes.

## If not the American flag, then the Cuban flag?

A visit to the Houston campaign headquarters of Obama for President offers a brutally severe view into Obama's allegiances, or at least those of his campaign staff.

Tacked up on the wall in Obama HQ was a Cuban flag with the image of Che Guevara silk-screened over it. Che worship is a phase that many hard-left activists go through in adolescence. But they usually get over this youthful indiscretion when they learn what a corrupt, repressive, killjoy regime Che and Fidel straddled the Cuban people with for decades.

That Obama's staffers would still worship the Marxist, America-hating Che while trying to win the American presidency calls into question the very legitimacy of Obama's campaign. When news of the Che-lover flag leaked into the press, Obama could have diffused the whole issue with a quick statement to the press. A simple disavowal would have been sufficient. After all, a candidate can't keep tabs on every single whack job who goes to work for him.

But Obama said nothing. Houston, we have a problem.

## Did Obama really find himself an even worse pastor?

After the Reverend Wright fiasco, one might expect Obama to find himself a prude of a pastor. So who did he choose?

Obama remained loyal to Trinity United with its two new pastors—each pieces of work themselves. The first is Otis Moss III, who Obama calls *"a wonderful young pastor."* [88] Unlike his predecessor, the Reverend Moss III doesn't hate his country or white people. He's more of a lover … of thugs, felons, and sexual deviants. In one of his sermons, inconveniently posted to YouTube, the Reverend Moss III admonishes the simple-minded among us for not reveling in the greatness of common street thugs:

> There are times when our prejudice keeps us from hearing ghetto prophets, who preach a brand of thug theology which keeps us from hearing the truth from their lips because of their course language and ragged subject-verb agreement.

As an example of the ghetto prophets we should seek heed, the Reverend Moss III cites Tupac Shakur. Before being gunned down in Las Vegas, the rapper Shakur had done time for numerous counts of sexual assault, assault and battery, and carrying a concealed weapon. But we should emulate Shakur, Obama's new pastor insists.

In seeking scriptural support for his bold views, the Reverend Moss III offers up evidence (that must have slipped past the rest of us) that the biblical patriarch *"Abraham was a pimp"* and Noah and Moses *"thugs."* Bringing his argument full circle, the Reverend Moss III tells congregants that anyone who doesn't recognize that the rapper Shakur is a prophet and biblical figures are thugs is confined by *"bourgeois paradigms."* Self-righteously, he rests his case.

The Reverend Moss III is a relative newcomer to Obama's church, but not so the Reverend Michael Pfleger, who has a friendship with Obama dating back twenty years. Reverend Pfleger fashions himself more in the Reverend Wright mode, exposing *"white entitlement and supremacy wherever it raises its head."* [89]

Reverend Pfleger found exactly that, he claimed, in Hillary's primary campaign. Up at the pulpit, the pews filled with families, Pfleger launched into full blather on Hillary:

> I really believe that she just always thought, 'This is mine! I'm Bill's wife, I'm white, and this is mine! I just gotta get up and step into the plate.' And then out of nowhere came, 'Hey, I'm Barack Obama,' and she said,

*'Oh, damn! Where did you come from? I'm white! I'm entitled! There's a black man stealing my show!'*

Unfortunately for Pfleger, there were also video cameras in the church that day. And soon a clip on YouTube told the rest of the nation what everyone in south Chicago knows: Jeremiah Wright is not an outlier. He is merely one of many crazy uncles in Obama's crowded attic.

If a Presidential contender has taken moral and spiritual guidance in such a perverse format, what kind of moral leadership would he provide the nation? Again we cringe.

When Bill Clinton was caught with Monica Lewinsky, an immoral (and, in fact, amoral) message was sent out to everyone of this country, and parents were stuck trying to explain adult themes to their young children. It was a low and embarrassing moment in our nation's history, and it contributed mightily to the coarsening of American culture.

Now what would parents be forced to tell their children if the President endorses the criminal behavior of street thugs and trashes time-honored prophets?

Obama's supporters will insist that the candidate's choice of churches bears not in the least on his ability to lead. With the disdain that liberals have for organized religion, they may believe what they say. But they are wrong. Obama's choice of churches tells us precisely what kinds of choices Obama would make as President.

## One endorsement you won't find on Obama's website.

Shaaban Abdel Rahim has pledged his support for Obama's candidacy. Haven't heard of Shaabolla, as his pals call him? Perhaps that's because you missed his 2000 song release, *"I Hate Israel,"* which didn't get as much play at he'd hoped.

Other Shaabolla hits include a tribute to bin Laden with the catchy chorus, "Bin Bin Bin Bin Bin Bin Laden." Then there was *"Hey People, It Was Only a Tower"* in 2001, *"Don't Hit Iraq"* in 2003, and *"We Are All Out of Patience"* in 2006 when he spoke of the Muslim world's wrath and impending revenge over a cartoon of Mohammed.

Shaabolla told a Lebanese newspaper[90] that Obama is *"a good man, and kindhearted."* We suspect Obama didn't seek Shaabolla's support. But it does affirm Obama's own contention that if he wins, it will change how the rest of the world looks at America.

## Wasn't about race, until black leaders made it so.

Obama's devolution from a candidate who happens to be black, to the black candidate, was both surprising and unavoidable.

The truth is, America has been ready for a candidate who happens to be black for more than a decade. Recall the excitement for a Colin Powell candidacy back in 1995. Polling figures at one point had him beating President Clinton by a 10-point margin.[91]

Obama began his race for the Presidency bathed in an excitement similar to Powell's. Both men brought a charisma and personal story that put the old racial concerns to rest. Both men had excelled in a "white" world. Powell in the U.S. Army, Obama at Harvard Law School. Both men embodied the can-do optimism Americans prize. But there the comparison abruptly stopped.

As chairman of the Joint Chiefs of Staff, Powell had run the armed forces of the most powerful nation on earth and directed a successful war in a time when America's ability to do so was under question. In evicting the Iraqi army from Kuwait, Powell put his executive talents on display. And we all applauded.

When Obama announced for the Presidency, he had no such accomplishments to point to. This lack of experience does not by itself disqualify Obama for the Presidency. But it does require the asking of earnest questions in hopes of gaining insight into the leadership talents Obama would muster if he were elevated as a young inexperienced man into the Oval Office.

In full disclosure, we'll admit that our first impressions of Obama were quite favorable. Like many people, we were genuinely impressed with Obama's first big national speech at the Democratic National Convention in Boston in 2004. We thought to ourselves and wrote at the time:

> *Here's the new face of the Democratic Party—a new generation leader, free from the shackles of the past, eloquent, inspiring—a long overdue return to principled leadership on the Democratic side of the aisle.*

And then we began looking at precisely what Obama had been doing on his side of the aisle and were given our first peek at the man behind the mask. We found no galvanizing political idea, just an audacious claim to hopefulness and a commitment to "change." By the evidence of his slight political record, Obama barely got passing marks. None of which matters. This race is about race.

It didn't start out that way, and we don't believe that Obama, to his credit, wanted it to be about race. Not entirely, anyway. But early on **Obama was betrayed by his own black brothers who saw his candidacy as a platform to air their countless grievances.** He was penned in and pinned down. So, early on, Obama and his handlers began a delicate balancing act— just enough black, just enough white—in hopes of surviving what promised to be a grueling campaign.

Yes, this race is about race now. It's the subject nobody wants to confront with any real honesty. There's too much back story, too much guilt. So the conversation is too often conducted in a code—with words that have been washed of meaning.

Well, we have no problems venturing honestly down this path. We agree with columnist Tony Blankley that there have been *"two conversations about race"* in this country for too long:

> *…a polite public one that uses euphemisms or evasions about race and a nasty private one that is likely to dredge*

*up the worst within us—the conversation that won't be on television but will be on the Internet and on the subway and wherever people congregate to chat.*[92]

The more honest the public conversation, Blankley believes, the more courteous the private conversation can be. So we'll speak in honest terms, and hope that it has a calming effect on the private conversation.

For honesty, we admire the writings of the black liberal Bob Herbert. In *The New York Times* Herbert lamented the irony of the "new slavery" blacks have sold themselves into:

*One of the cruelest aspects of slavery was the way it wrenched apart black families, separating husbands from wives and children from their parents. It is ironic, to say the least, that now, nearly a century and a half after the Emancipation Proclamation, much of the most devastating damage to black families, and especially black children, is self-inflicted.*[93]

Some more honesty comes from another liberal with impeccable credentials, Geraldine Ferraro. She would have been Vice President if Walter Mondale had been a viable candidate. Ferraro spoke honestly, saying:

*If Obama was a white man, he would not be in this position.*

And oh how the liberal media pounced. Ferraro was taken out to the woodshed. All because she had the audacity of honesty. Of course Obama wouldn't be a Presidential contender if he was white. No record, no name recognition, no platform. Nothing but hope. And audacity. No white man would dare run on "hope" alone. Obama knows all this—he knows it better than anyone. For while new to the national stage, he is no fool.

In his carefully crafted memoirs, written at an age where many are still struggling in graduate school, Obama talked of the difficulty he had in overcoming race, how it has been a tremendous liability for him, when surely he knows that his blackness is his ticket. Moreover, he has been willing to use it. Saying at a fundraiser on June 20, 2008 in Jacksonville, Florida:

> We know what kind of campaign they're going to run. They're going to try to make you afraid. They're going to try to make you afraid of me. 'He's young and inexperienced and he's got a funny name. And did I mention he's black?'

Obama is injecting race front and center as his counter to any questions about his record, policies or resume.

## "Race" is now the drama that Obama needs.

Obama's dark skin allows the dream weavers to spin their fables into allegory. As *Lord of the Rings* was to the World Wars, and *Wizard of Oz* to Wicked Government, *Barack Hussein Obama* is to Racial Harmony.

Now there's a storyline for the people!

Who wants to hear about budget deficits and education reform when we can obsess on America's tortured racial past? Why delve into the sticky issues of immigration and healthcare when we can throw off the yoke of racial hatreds? In Obama there is the promise of finally resolving great injustices, and in so doing, playing a role in destiny's unfolding. Indeed, for many Americans of all races, Obama is just too good an opportunity to pass up.

Laying the groundwork for this racially charged drama was not easy, and required that Obama follow a time-tested formula. **It is a formula that famous blacks such as Louis Armstrong, Bill Cosby and Oprah Winfrey have followed to obtain their goals.** Shelby Steele writes that blacks like Obama have to strike a bargain with whites:

> Bargaining is a mask that blacks can wear in the American mainstream, one that enables them to put whites at their ease. This mask diffuses the anxiety that goes along with

*being white in a multiracial society. Bargainers make the subliminal promise to whites not to shame them with America's history of racism, on the condition that they will not hold the bargainer's race against him.*[94]

If you accept this thinking, then you see how Obama's lightspeed hurtling of other more qualified Democrats in the primaries owes less to who he is, than to a hunger among sensitive white Americans for the forgiveness of their racial sins.

Steele writes how Louis Armstrong adapted the iconic mask of the black minstrel tradition. His big beaming smile, the reflexive bowing, the exaggerated graciousness—it told white audiences of the time that he, Louis Armstrong, did not presume to be their equal.[95]

Later Bill Cosby struck a similar bargain with white America. He made it clear from the start that he was a comedian and no more, and that if good white families tuned into his show each week they wouldn't have the awful stain of white racism rubbed in their face. When Cosby later tossed off his mask and set about berating a generation of black men for their many failures, he broke the bargain, and became an instant pariah among liberal blacks and whites "who didn't want no truth-telling going on."

The next big black bargainer was Oprah Winfrey. Her success came entirely from exploiting the feelings of helplessness that many people experience. By feeling their pain and blaming the Man five days a week, she built a phenomenally successful empire. Never once did she remove the mask, or even come close to admitting the truth that blacks could only improve their lot if blacks like all other members of the human race began to take responsibility for their actions.

After all, wasn't it the taking of responsibility that launched the civil rights movement? Surely Oprah knows the answer to that question. But she knows, too, that if she peels away the mask she loses her iconic place in American society.

As for the role that Oprah is playing in Obama's campaign—those developments are coming in just a few pages.

## Obama Unmasked

The woman closest to Obama knows how to play the race game, as well. Michelle Obama has stumbled more than once—being new to the national stage. But she knows her role. She knows she cannot be a smooth bargainer like Oprah Winfrey, or an abrasive challenger like Jesse Jackson. She must tow a middle road, playing the race card with a gentle finesse. And so she informed us in a 60 Minutes interview:

> *Barack is black. He can be shot on the way to the gas station.*[96]

Whoa! Tracing the path of Obama's life, it is hard to imagine there was ever a chance of him getting shot—presumably by some gun-toting, knuckle-dragging white boy—on the way to the gas station. There was certainly good odds of him being shot or roughed-up by black hoodlums on the mean streets of South Chicago. But no matter. **Michelle was playing to the guilt white liberals feel when confronted with intelligent blacks. Her manipulation was exquisitely executed.** Her deed was done. There would be no back-biting from liberals after that "can get shot" comment. Obama was in the clear—at least for awhile.

So we have all these blacks, wearing all these masks, playing all these iconic figures. And all is fine, for a while. But as time passes, these people behind their masks are no longer visible to us as human beings. We got to know them with their masks in place. That is all we know of them. Obama himself has spoken to this condition:

> *I serve as a blank screen on which people of vastly different political stripes project their own views...*

Everyone is content to enjoy the performance of the masked man, as long as it remains a performance. **But when it becomes serious, when the masked man runs for President, then we shift in our expectations. We want to learn more, to look behind the mask.** So we begin in earnest to peel away the mask. We begin to see the real man, and the minute we do, something happens

We see the man for who he really is.  We see his quirks of character and foibles.  He is now ruined for us as an icon.  He is no longer a "blank screen."  For blacks and for whites, he is ruined for different reasons.

To keep liberal blacks happy, Obama must exaggerate black victimization.  He must blame high illegitimacy rates, high crime rates, and high family collapse rates on the long history of white oppression.  Many bright black people reject these tired racial stereotypes, but those bright people don't hold leadership roles in Chicago politics, or in national politics.  Not on the Democratic side of the aisle, anyway.  Obama must insist that a wise and benevolent government will step in and solve all their problems.  Obama must heap praise on the black nationalist preachers and violent radicals who helped launch him into the national spotlight.

But now in the spotlight, he must also keep whites happy.  To do this, Obama must speak of the opportunity and promise our nation offers.  He must praise families for bucking the odds and lifting themselves up by their bootstraps.  And, most importantly, he must appear the model of decency.

These two visions that Obama must paint—one to black audiences and another to white audiences—are completely at odds with each other. **When they clash, Obama's mask cracks.** A hairline at first, then a sustained break … like the one sustained at the nexus of the Don Imus and Duke Lacrosse stories.

## Stuck between Don Imus and a Lacrosse stick.

The two most racially charged news stories of recent were radio show host Don Imus's remarks about the Rutgers women's basketball team, and the Duke lacrosse rape case.  Since both of these stories were, on face value, about whites abusing blacks, every black leader including Obama pounded the podium and staked out their positions in the media.  What positions did Obama take?

When Don Imus called the lady ballplayers *"nappy head-ed hos,"* Obama roundly condemned the remarks and the man. Imus was out of line, and Obama was correct to condemn him. Though given all the vitriol the Reverend Wright had spewed for years, Obama may have wondered what all the fuss was about. But we digress.

When a bunch of left-wing professors and hard-core feminists at Duke teamed with an ambitious prosecutor to falsely accuse white members of the lacrosse team of raping a young black dancer, Obama said nothing. Three young white men were being demonized in the national news. There were lies being told about the evidence against the men. Their civil rights were being repeatedly violated. Three Congressmen demanded in December 2006 that U.S. Attorney General Gonzales conduct a thorough investigation of the prosecutor's conduct. As for Obama, he did nothing except to respond to a letter from a constituent twelve months after the scandal first broke, and in that letter tell the constituent that an *"independent inquiry is needed."* [97]

The takeaway here? Don Imus can be condemned because the victims were black; the Duke prosecutor, professors and feminists cannot be condemned because the victims were white. Doesn't get more transparently racist than that. It is the reason that in the end, white voters will question if Obama's candidacy is any different from Al Sharpton's or Jesse Jackson's.

## Is Obama really any different?

Like Al Sharpton and Jesse Jackson before him, Obama's run at the Presidency is based more on the manipulation of white guilt than on substance. Sharpton and Jackson weren't as smooth as Obama, but that kind of smoothness is only skin deep. In the end, is there any real difference between the three men?

# 11.  Are We In For The Nastiest Election Yet?

Everyone talks about returning civility to politics, but no-body does anything about it.  Fact is, politics has been a rough and tumble sport since the Greeks gave us modern democracy around 508 BC.  Fierce passions should be ignited in politics—and why not?  Would we be governed by people with whom we disagree?  Would we take a hands-off approach to social order?  No, so we fight.

At least in this country we fight with words, for the most part.  In the many countries that liberals are constantly seeking approval from, there is a greater tendency to resolve political differences with fire hoses, bullet sprays and bloody coups.  In America we have a rich tradition of employing truth and lies.  It is the electorate's duty to distinguish between the two, and act in their own and the nation's best interests.

These are rather obvious notions, yet so often lost on the clamoring voices of the Left.  **They will, for example, insist on some wild global income redistribution and when everyone doesn't chime in with *"Cool, dude!"*, their feelings will be hurt**, that hurt will turn to anger, that anger will steal all reason, (*"those God-loving-Bush-adoring-devils on the right started it all, you know!"*) and now it's nasty time.

One finds greater decorum in professional wrestling.

Another thing loudmouthed liberals don't understand is that when it comes to vicious character assassination, they're tops.  There's a good reason for this.  It's the same reason that 95% of the creative talent in Hollywood is politically liberal.  (Our apologies to Joel Surnow and the handful of conservative talents in Hollywood—we know you exist, and love your work.)  But the *creative* storytelling impulse is one of rebellion, revolution, radical-ism—the stuff of inspired storytelling, but not necessarily inspired

151

politics. When it comes to making-up stories about good and evil, the writers and producers in Hollywood are without peer. And one of the best is David Geffen.

# The invisible hand of David Geffen.

Unlike Obama, Geffen has a resume: One of the most successful record producers of all-time; co-founder with Steven Spielberg and Jeffrey Katzenberg of DreamWorks Studios; on the Forbes list of 400 richest Americans with an estimated net worth of $6 billion; openly gay and a prickly perfectionist who gets what he wants (he tried to buy the *Los Angeles Times* in 2007 for $2 billion).

Geffen has exercised more influence over the entertainment industry than perhaps any living person. As he showed in movie hits such as *Saving Private Ryan, Gladiator* and *Beetlejuice,* he can make us laugh and wonder, weep with tears and yes, follow him into the polls to vote for Obama.

Some call Geffen a "pied piper" and a biography *The Operator: David Geffen Builds, Buys, and Sells the New Hollywood* portrayed him as saint, visionary and absolute maniac who will do anything to seal the deal. In this election, the tinseltown titan will be sealing the deal for Obama at a level of sophistication never seen before.

**We have been tracking Geffen's activities** as closely as possible—not an easy task, so much is hidden. We've uncovered plans **to launch a "November Surprise" to complement the "October Surprise" that his financial counterpart George Soros is reported to be launching** (outlined back in Chapter 8) to lock-in an Obama victory.

In short, we expect a Soros October Surprise and a Geffen November Surprise—a one two punch for the "Big Election Fight."

Geffen was first a friend and fundraising ally of the Clintons. But the relationship was always one of convenience. Geffen was a top packager in Hollywood—he could put anything together, including boatloads of cash for liberal politicians. But privately he chafed at the one-way street relationships the Clintons were famous for. It was always about the Clintons.

So Geffen had long been eager for a less self-centered liberal, someone he could *proudly* support. When Obama began putting out feelers even before announcing his candidacy for President, Geffen made it clear that his dance card was open. When Obama officially launched, Geffen wasted little time in deserting Hillary for President.

Hillary knew the score. She immediately lashed out at Geffen with a venomous fury brutal even by Hillary's standards. Pundits said she was sending a message to other would-be deserters. But the larger reason for her anger: she was very aware of the election-tipping powers Geffen possesses, and intends to exercise.

Geffen's first big foray for Team Obama was a fundraiser that shoveled $1.3 million into Obama's campaign coffers. Not bad for a night's work, but that was just the public "face" of Geffen's schemes. It was his **conversations with big-name celebrities and producers at that event that will unfold into political activism in November**, in what promises to be the biggest crossover of entertainment and politics in American history.

## Key intel on the "November Surprise."

Geffen, like Soros, is taking no chances and has repeatedly dubbed his efforts with the code name C3. We are guessing that it stands for "**Campaign Crush Conservatives**." He is planning a 3-phase strategy to energize younger voters, appeal to their base instincts, and ensure they actually remember to vote on Election Day. It's a tall order, but one that was planned in late 2007 and is already being executed, according to a Hollywood-based source who witnessed the plans in their early stages.

This source has made a good living as a screenwriter in Hollywood, and has not once in 17 years of steady employment in the movie business revealed that she is an independent voter, entering each election open-minded to candidates of both parties, making her final voting decision based on the issues. This kind of deviant behavior is simply not tolerated in Hollywood proper, and so the writer has kept her opinions to herself.

Whenever asked about politics, she has joked that *"nobody in their right mind would ever vote for a Republican."* It's the kind of line that earns hoots in Hollywood, and it has satisfied her fellow workers for years without revealing any real truth.

The intel we have from this source is uncorroborated, and thus potentially unreliable. But in the conversations we had with this responsible, married mother of three at the Urth Caffé on Melrose Avenue in Los Angeles led us to believe that if her "scenario of unfolding events" doesn't hit the bullseye exactly, it hits close. This is her story:

> *I was approached by David [Geffen] about writing a script about 'a group of mangled and broken Iraq War vets who tell of the wretched horrors they've seen, and how it's got to change.'*

Such a storyline was consistent with the anti-war biopics that Geffen had produced in recent years, so the writer didn't question it in the least. And only a fool would turn down an opportunity to work with Geffen. So she took the job, without hesitation. The contract she was asked to sign carried an especially lengthy confidentiality proviso—but she had signed similar contracts countless times.

A month later by appointment, the writer met with Geffen to review her first draft. While waiting outside his office for the meeting to begin, she overhead him talking on the phone, saying *"C3 is coming along"* and *"the second phase is out in my lobby now."*

The writer thought nothing of his words—big Hollywood producers often speak in code, and of multiple phases and sequels. But once in his office, pitching her story as far as she'd developed it, Geffen began asking questions that left her perplexed:

*David had a song in his head, a 'we are the world' type ditty with literally hundreds of celebrity actors all performing in it. He wanted to know how I might integrate the song into my storyline. I joked that I wasn't doing 'Springtime for Hitler' but he didn't laugh...*

Instead, Geffen shot her an 'I don't suffer fools' glare. And she promised to consider his idea and have an answer the next day. Then Geffen asked her opinion on a seemingly unrelated matter:

*David asked if I thought there would ever come a day when the people of this country would be so 'browned off' by all the political B.S. that they'd call a national strike? It was an interesting question, and not wanting to let him down a second time, I said 'Yes, and I think that time is now; there ought to be a national strike, and on a day that matters.'*

She could see a light bulb flashing on in Geffen's mind. The very next day, however, she was fired. No explanation. No final payment. It was a breach of contract, not uncommon in Hollywood, especially from self-important moguls like Geffen. But it was this breach that so angered the screenwriter, she found us.

# The 3-phase strategy planned for November.

When we first met, she had already salved her anger by piecing together a plausible 3-phase scenario. She knew that Geffen was on board the Obama campaign. She figured Geffen was producing the 3-phase campaign offensive for Obama:

1. **A major hit song to warn of the danger America faces**
2. **A war vet movie to discredit Republican rule**
3. **A national strike to mobilize citizens to vote Obama**

Phase 1 would be the easiest to pull off. Geffen could rip through his rolodex and with a half day's work have several hundred of America's most beloved celebrities lined up for a gala studio performance of a song that 5,000 radio stations in major markets could be guaranteed to play five to ten times a day. The song would build on he phenomenal success of the first song performed for Obama by the group Black Eyed Peas, titled *"Yes We Can!"* and featuring loads of celebrities.

As for the war vet movie, Geffen had asked her to write it with a bit of melodrama, as if it were a stageplay. Or maybe, just maybe, it was a traveling show with the actors' lines loosely scripted. A show that could go into cities across America late in the election, telling of the hellish mistake of Iraq, and how no more American blood must be shed by Republicans. Geffen said this was Phase 2; the song was probably Phase 1 and it would set up the "disgruntled vet tour" as Phase 2.

That left Phase 3, a national strike—but when? How about on Election Day itself! And not just any strike, but a call on all Americans to walk out of their classrooms, out of their workplaces, out of their homes—and vote for Obama. Civil disobedience at its best. A national "civil rights" type strike for everyone who missed the real marches. And how better to turn out the younger voters than with celebrity cover? *"Tom Hanks said I couldn't come to work today"* could be a powerful driver.

As this screenwriter laid out her scenario, we sat flabbergasted. Could such a crazy plot be possible? Or was she just angry at Geffen, and spinning yarns in hopes we would print them and fatally disgrace Geffen? Surely if we did print her speculations, he would know the source. Breached contract or not, he could make her life miserable. We pointed this out to her, and she responded:

> *C'est la vie! I've spent too long in this vapid town anyway. When I see this kind of behind-the-scene manipulation, I wretch! Our country is too important to let storytellers run it.*

No disagreement there.

Soon we'll know exactly what Geffen and his many creative allies have planned for the 2008 Presidential election. And perhaps by printing Geffen's plans here, we'll help squash them in time to make a difference.

# Hollywood is already throwing its talent around.

Early in the race, actors Robert DeNiro, Chris Rock, Forest Whitaker, Scarlett Johansson and many other entertainment talents publicly pledged their support for Obama.

Tom Hanks posted a video on his MySpace page. In that perfectly practiced self-deprecating way of his, he said that *"as an official celebrity, I know my endorsement has just made your mind up for you."*

Mr. Hanks is no fool. He knows that by downplaying the value of his endorsement he actually enhances its influence among younger voters. Mr. Hanks added that he was supporting Obama because of the "character and vision" Obama has brought to this campaign. We applaud Mr. Hanks his honesty—lacking credentials, character and vision are truly the only things Obama has to offer.

Another early endorsement came from Stevie Wonder. The talented musician warmed-up the crowd for Obama in Indianapolis. After playing his hit *"Signed, Sealed, Delivered I'm Yours,"* Mr. Wonder told the crowd that his endorsement of Obama comes from *"a man who has the vision of the heart because I am color free."*

Few Hollywood starlets have made a bigger splash in their loving adoration for Obama than Scarlett Johansson, star of *The Other Boleyn Girl, The Nanny Diaries, Donkey Punch, Veggies for Sloth, A Piece of the Action, Toyz in the Hood, The Black Dahlia, The Perfect Score* and other films suggesting a lifetime spent preparing for the role of "candidate's favorite girl."

Scarlett and Barack have been quite the email pals during the campaign, and she often comforts him when he's had a tough day:

> *Someone like the Senator who is constantly traveling and constantly 'on'... how can he return these personal emails?*[98]

Scarlett has said that she is "*engaged*" to Obama and that "*my heart belongs to Barack.*" The controversy raised so many eyebrows, even the late-night comedians took their shots. This one from Jay Leno:

> *So you've got a 23-year-old gorgeous, blonde actress emailing a married Presidential candidate. Well, what could go wrong there, huh?*

Though not Hollywood celebrities *per se*, those two merry entertainers Ben & Jerry have also been swept up in Obama-mania and are apparently staking the profits of their ice cream empire on an Obama victory. They have endorsed Obama with a new flavor. Says a blogger at *The Black Republican*:

> *It couldn't be chocolate. That would be racist. It couldn't contain Oreo cookies, either. That would just be wrong. It couldn't contain fruit, because that might offend the gays. [It] couldn't contain nuts because it might offend the crazy. I guess he'll just be selling a big bucket of frozen cream. For some reason, this seems like the perfect metaphor for the Obama campaign; he's all about change, but won't tell us what that change is.*[99]

We can imagine all the politically astute of Hollywood turning out for the Obama cause.

Certainly, George Clooney will be there to remind us that "*the government itself is running exactly like the Sopranos... going to kill a lot of innocent people.*"

Jessica *"I'm ashamed of the United States"* Lange can be counted on to join with Michelle Obama in the refrain, *"We're finally proud of the United States."*

And what's a songfest without Martin Sheen up on risers so we can see him. Mr. Sheen is a consummate pro at remembering the lines he's told to read. So this go-round, we can expect him to reprise his old crowd pleaser, and inform us that *"John McCain is like a bad comic working the crowd, a moron."*

Will we see the talented film director, Robert Altman, appearing at Obama's events? Like Obama, he has an aversion to the displays of patriotism and has announced, *"When I see an American flag flying, it's a joke."* Maybe they'll hide him in the back row.

These sages of Hollywood have never had to answer for their role in driving up oil prices. Perhaps now they could. Recall how, in the last election, novelist Gore Vidal called 9/11 a just payback for our attacks on other nations. Novelist Tom Robbins called the U.S. an *"adolescent bully, a pubescent punk...good to have our butts kicked."* The deep-thinking Woody Harrelson admonished, *"There can be no more deaths, no transfusions of blood for oil."* Singer Barbra Streisand informed us, *"The real reason we are invading Iraq now...oil."* And Dustin Hoffman couldn't but agree, *"This war is about...hegemony, money, power, and oil."* All of these acting talents should be waving pom-poms for Obama to win, but we'd like them and Obama to answer a few questions for us first.

If those evil-geniuses in the White House were so hell-bent on getting cheap oil, how did they fail so miserably and why are we stuck with $4 plus a gallon fuel?

Why do we spend so much political and financial capital defending Israel (which has no oil) against the Arab states (which are swimming in oil)?

Why did we slap an oil embargo on Iraq while Saddam was still in power?

Why do we boycott oil sales from Iran, while Europeans buy all they can?

The hard fact is – Iraq was producing about two million barrels of oil a day against a global oil output of 76 million barrels. So are we to believe that the "war on terror" in Iraq is being fought over 3% of the world's oil production?

Wrong script, guys.

We understand the difficulty all the beautiful people in Hollywood face. George Bush did an awful job of selling our occupation of Iraq, and for that he took heaps of deserved criticism. But Bush isn't in this race. Two Senators are. Both of them have been in Washington during this oil crisis. Focus on that.

To all the beautiful people in Hollywood who will turn out for Obama, know that we love watching you up on the big screen, we love listening to your songs, and you do touch a deep chord in all of us who yearn for peace. But know, too, that you are out of touch with one important reality:

While you sing your sweet songs, we have Islamic fascists singing of jihad and attacking Americans and glorifying the day that "American bodies will pile up in bags." That's a problem for a lot of us. That's why good and sensible people were happy when President Bush took this war to the enemy far from America's shore. That wasn't some cheap song lyric, that was the President protecting America.

What has Obama done to protect America? Not a thing.

## The biggest wild card of all—Oprah.

More than any other celebrity, Oprah Winfrey has the potential to turn her outreach empire into a veritable typhoon of election-day support for Obama. She has been cautious in issuing firm political endorsements in the past, to her credit. But this race will be different.

Both Oprah and Obama have attended the same church, both have a wonderful black-American story to tell. So naturally Oprah urged millions of adoring fans to purchase the book of an unknown state Senator from Illinois back in 2006. That little urging sent his book leaping off the shelves, and planted him on the national radar.

"Oprah-Obama '08" t-shirts are prized possessions in liberal circles and selling at a brisk clip. While nobody thinks it likely, if Obama did select Oprah for a running mate if would rank as the most unusual ticket in American history (though it does lend itself to some interesting Cabinet appointments – Dr. Phil as Secretary of Sensitivity, for example).

However Oprah uses her TV pulpit on Obama's behalf in the waning days of the campaign, you know it will be engaging and results-producing. A lot of daytime TV watchers who wouldn't ordinarily lift their sorry selves off the couch to vote will be mobilized to actually get out and vote on election day. That they won't have the foggiest idea what they're voting for will be immaterial. Oprah told 'em. End of story.

With Oprah on board, Geffen pulling strings behind the scenes, Hollywood talent strutting before the cameras on cue, there will emerge a dazzling confluence of entertainment and politics. We'll see celebrities trying to act cerebral. We'll see fine storytelling. We'll see Obama...

# Running on aura.

Obama is being advised by his Hollywood handlers to continue touting his total lack of relevant experience. Their private polling at regular intervals throughout the primary campaign has confirmed that it is precisely his absence of executive and legislative experience that appeals most to liberal voters. Obama is admired among liberals not for his works, but for his words. One of Obama's admirers, liberal commentator Ezra Klein, described Obama's appeal like this:

> *Obama's finest speeches do not excite. They do not inform. They don't even really inspire. They elevate. They enmesh you in a grander moment, as if history has stopped flowing passively by, and, just for an*

*instant, contracted around you, made you aware of its presence, and your role in it. He is not the word made flesh, but the triumph of word over flesh, over color, over despair.*[100]

Obama's speeches have been crafted to transcend politics with all of its messy position requirements. He has artfully positioned himself as an amorphous agent of change, hurtling himself against corrupt interests in Washington and politics-as-usual. He himself is the message. He is hope that people seek.

Obama's gift for elevating politics to a grander more spiritual level means that he can sidestep the nitty-gritty of single issue politics, and run instead on aura—on his oneness with all things beautiful.

## He's JFK, he's MLK, why he's Mary Kay!

Obama's handlers are of course ecstatic that they can run on aura, because it plays to their strengths. They can compare Obama to Gandhi; they can sell him as a Black Jesus; they can volley back and forth between MLK and JFK comparisons and never have to fret over any pesky examinations of the many glaring discrepancies.

Who knows, they may even invoke Mary Kay—a white woman of the heartland who, like his dear Mom, struck out in pursuit of her dreams and left a colored path for generations to follow. Does a Mary Kay comparison sound absurd? Doesn't matter to Team Obama. He is the blank screen onto which they project their fondest hopes and aspirations. Riding the Obama aura can be a rush, you know.

Obama's handlers know this. They know they have a lock on the votes from the illusional *and* delusional Left. Their concern is with independent voters, principally the white male who must in this election choose between a candidate who is older and almost passé and a candidate who is too young and inexperienced.

Analysts agree that these white males may decide the election.

So in fashioning an acceptable appeal to this audience, Barack Hussein Obama shall be presented as the new John Fitzgerald Kennedy. If Jack's brother Teddy is strong enough on the heels of brain surgery, he will be trotted out to draw a compelling comparison between the two men. That's a bridge he would be foolish to cross, but oh well.

**Both JFK and BHO, we will be told, rose up quickly in elected politics and are the visionaries of their times.**

FACT IS, JFK had served six years in the U.S. House of Representatives and eight years in the U.S. Senate. BHO spent eight years in the Illinois State Senate representing one little slum in Chicago, then he spent two years in the U.S. Senate before launching his White House bid. As for the vision BHO brings to the job, we don't dispute it in the least. His eyesight appears perfectly fine.

**Both JFK and BHO both threw off the yoke of oppression and rose up in heroic service of their country.**

Apart from the obvious messianic undertones of this comparison, JFK was a genuine hero who nearly died in World War II. BHO may be lucky to have survived the mean streets of Chicago when he organized there—but the comparison is flimsy. As for tossing yokes, the jury is out. JFK's Catholicism was thought to be a handicap for him; BHO's ethnicity may be a handicap, but it may be a benefit in a nation that has mostly moved beyond old racial stigmas.

**BHO like JFK before him, we will be told, will make the hard decisions required to keep America safe in a dangerous world.**

FACT IS, JFK was hawkish on foreign policy. In his inaugural address in 1961, JFK let the nations of the world know, *"We shall pay any price, bear any burden, meet any hardship, support any friend, oppose any foe, in order to assure the survival and the success of liberty."* JFK's subsequent unwillingness to appease the Soviet Union brought our two nations to the brink of nuclear war.

Early in his campaign, BHO showed himself to be a foreign policy piker by saying what no U.S. President had ever been so naïve to say: That he would meet with any despot at any time or place in the name of peace. So the signal went out to our enemies worldwide—under BHO, America could be pushed around. In the weeks following BHO's declaration, leaders of countries at war with America endorsed BHO.

**BHO like JFK before him, we will be told, has an economic plan that will get America back on her feet.**

FACT IS, JFK supported a flight of tax cuts that ignited economic growth. BHO has pledged to raise our taxes because that's the only way, in his view, to get government under control.

**BHO like JFK before him, we will be told, will call on all Americans to band together in common cause to address the problems we all face as a united people.**

FACT IS, when JFK told us to ask what we could do for our country, he followed it up with a laundry list of things we could do. BHO was given an education by taxpayers; he went to work showing poor blacks how to collect food stamps; he is trying to send almost a trillion dollars in U.S. wealth to foreign nations. His entire adult life has been spent working an angle on government.

We can't imagine all of this flying with voters. So when the spotlight is on BHO at the Democratic National Convention, and the nation tunes-in in earnest, BHO will have some convincing to do.

## A convention speech like none before.

It is Obama's great fortune to be delivering the most important speech of his life—his acceptance address at the Democratic National Convention—on the night of August 28th. For it is the 45th anniversary of Martin Luther King Jr.'s *"I Have A Dream"* speech. Voters who didn't bite at the JFK-BHO parallels will now be treated to the MLK-BHO parallels.

In the media coverage that attends the speech, be prepared for the Densest Concentration of Similes in Recorded History. Obama will be found to be "like" MLK right down to his toes. It will be an orgy of fatuous comparisons owing everything to the color of the speaker and nothing to the content of the speech.

What do these two men have in common, really, beyond skin color?

MLK towered above centuries-old walls of racial hatred by speaking truth to all sides—no matter their skin color. BHO has a different message for each audience—based wholly on their racial composition. He has yet to challenge any remaining racial divisions in this country in any meaningful way—except to apologize for attending a racially bigoted church for twenty years. His standard stump speech to liberal audiences, about government being the solution to their every problem, is very different than the speeches MLK gave.

As Juan Williams, NPR journalist and author of many books on the civil rights, has written of Dr. King:

> ...he gloried in black people beating the odds to win equal rights by arming 'ourselves with dignity and self-respect.' He expressed regret that some black leaders reveled in grievance, malice and self-indulgent anger in place of a focus on strong families, education and love of God. Even in the days before Congress passed civil rights laws, King spoke to black Americans about the pride that comes from 'assuming primary responsibility' for achieving 'first class citizenship.'[101]

There was one sparkling moment in Obama's campaign, at a rally commemorating the 1965 Selma march for civil rights, when Obama stood tall at the podium and sounded like Dr. King himself.  He spoke of "taking personal responsibility" and "strengthening the family" and told his black audience to stop denying that life hasn't improved since Jim Crow.  **Obama went so far as to say:**

> *Government alone can't solve all those problems... it is not enough just to ask what the government can do for us...it's important for us to ask what we can do for ourselves.*[102]

**In this one speech he hit the high notes, but that was the last time.  So, what happened?**

It has been suggested that once blacks joined with desperate liberals in support of Obama's candidacy, he no longer needed to inspire the best in blacks; he now needed to pander to the worst.  He needed to promise big sweet welfare programs for black leaders to run.  He needed to look the other way at a 70% illegitimacy rate in the black community.  He needed to sit in Reverend Wright's pews and nod along with the angry race-baiter.  In short, he needed to put on the mask of a great man on an important quest—unfettered by his own inactivity on issues of race.

By sliding his advocacy from "personal responsibility" to "government solutions" his very credibility came into question.  His ability to provide genuine race-neutral leadership came under scrutiny.  And his agenda for the presidency became suspect.

**What would Dr. King have done?**

He would have ripped off that mask, marched out of that church, and spoken truth to all sides.  That's the kind of honesty we have a right to expect from our leaders, no matter their color.

# III. Will We End Up Living In An Obamanation?

Few Presidents get the conditions for governing they want. Early on, they are confronted with events that shape their tenure, like it or not. The next President will be called upon to make difficult decisions, some we can anticipate, some we cannot. The man who next assumes the mantle of leadership will be tested as perhaps none before. Are we ready to trust this state of affairs to young Mr. Obama? In this section we examine an Obama presidency.

# 12. Terrorists Thinking We Are Weak?

It takes seven years and more than $8 billion to build one aircraft carrier from the keel up.[103] It takes twenty years to prepare the man, or woman, who will captain that carrier. And it takes 5,000 crew members, from senior officers to fresh-faced recruits, to help put that carrier to sea. Such a carrier, the USS Gerald R. Ford, is now under construction in Hampton Roads, Virginia. It will be ready to join the fleet in 2015, replacing a carrier launched 47 years ago. Do we know that the USS Ford will be needed in 2015? No, we don't. But can we afford to bet against it?

Obama thinks so. According to his campaign literature, he is willing to let the USS Ford and many more of tomorrow's defense technologies, rust at the pier.

The decision to build the USS Ford was based on the concept of preparing America for the war to come by anticipating the evil designs of irrational madmen. It's always a tricky business, trying to anticipate future unknowns. But the inaugural oath to protect and defend the United States includes making certain that ships like the USS Ford are ready to sail into harm's way.

The chief executive's job requires forward thinking, realistic assessments of the world's threats, and the maturity to make judgments in the name of national defense, not political expediency.

A President who doesn't fully appreciate this stark reality, and who hasn't had any experience in military strategic planning, is going to find himself in deep trouble when he finds his strategic armories empty in the face of an advancing enemy.

This is the situation George Bush found himself in on 9/11. Bill Clinton had systematically gutted the military for eight long years, and when our nation needed senior intelligence operatives to go to work immediately, we had only a skeleton crew to deploy.

Today, after stretching our armed services through two major conflicts, our military troop levels are at their lowest in decades. And the threats against our country are pushing our professional forces to their limits. Our enemies know this. They are watching. Calculating. Playing "what-if?" scenarios—all of which end with the United States on the losing end of conflict…or so the enemy hopes.

The only thing standing between their successful war-gaming and ours is a resolute President who is determined to stay one step ahead of all the bad boys hanging around the global water cooler these days.

Could that leader be Obama?

**Late on the night of January 20, 2009, the next Commander in Chief will head from the inaugural podium, parade, and festivities to the Oval Office where he will be met by a national security staff ready with the latest "threat briefing."** On his desk, they will place a thick binder of reports, each focusing on real or emerging threats to our national security. In the quiet of the Oval Office, in the presence of stern-faced, deadly serious briefers and advisors, Barack Hussein Obama, should he be the next President, will come face-to-face with reality.

## Threats our next President will face.

A review of Obama's national defense TV ads offers insight into his preparedness to meet today's and tomorrow's defense realities. In one TV commercial, Obama claims:[104]

1. I'm the only major candidate who opposed this war from the beginning, and as President, I will end it.

2. I will cut tens of billions of dollars in wasteful spending.

3. I will cut investments in unproven missile defense systems.

4. I will not weaponize space.

5. I will slow our development of future combat systems.

6. And I will institute an independent defense review board to ensure that the quadrennial defense review is not used to justify unnecessary spending.

7. I will set a goal of a world without nuclear weapons.

8. To seek that goal, I will not develop new nuclear weapons.

9. I will seek a global ban on the production of fissile material.

10. And I will negotiate with Russia to take our ICBMs off hair-trigger alert and to achieve deep cuts in our nuclear program.

## Item 1: I'm the only major candidate who opposed this war from the beginning, and as President, I will end it.

Obama wasn't even a member of the U.S. Senate when the war began. He had no national-level background briefings or access to classified information with which to make an informed decision. Had he been in the Senate, would he have made the same decision with the information available to other Senators? It's an irrelevant question.

He also wasn't in the Senate on September 11, 2001, and he didn't look out his Senate office window at smoke rising from the Pentagon while on the television in his office the World Trade Center collapsed and a field in Pennsylvania became an instant graveyard.

Surely Obama was stunned by the carnage of 9/11, but four years elapsed before he took office, and during that time, hard decisions were being made about how, where, and when

America's servicemen and women would engage the enemy. Obama was not part of that process.

He wasn't in the White House, agonizing over the loss of civilian life, or weighing the lives of our best young men and women who would soon be directly in the line of fire. He wasn't on the Senate Armed Services Committee, sifting through staff recommendations. He wasn't a former prisoner of war, fully appreciating the value of freedom and fearful for our security. He wasn't even a veteran with first-hand experience of what was about to be asked of soldiers, airmen, Marines, sailors, and Coastguardsmen in the years ahead.

The second part of Obama's sentence, "as President, I will end it," is all hubris. It insults our intelligence. If only he'd said, "as President, I will work toward ending it," or even better, "as President, I will make every effort to work with the military, our allies, and the Congress, to bring the war to an end" then he might have opened a door to reality. But no, "I will end it," is what he said, as if, like Moses parting the waters, he alone has the power to spread his mighty arms and conclude the conflict.

Add "Moses" to the list of Obama's messianic comparisons.

Iranian mullahs are licking their whiskers at the possibility a President Obama would withdraw American troops from Iraq, opening the door to wholesale slaughter, retribution and chaos. They have not forgotten that Iraq drew a lot of Iranian blood in their 1980s war, and revenge lasts a long time in the Middle East.

Iran's nutcase President, Mahmoud Ahmadinejad, is quite capable of working with Iraqi rogue cleric Moktada al-Sadr, the PLO, al-Qaeda, North Korea, Cuba, Venezuela and any other thug ruler and regime he can drag in to foment Iraqi civil war and further destabilize the Middle East. In ending the war, Obama would be triggering a new war that makes this one look like a Girl Scout campout.

## Item 2: I will cut tens of billions of dollars in wasteful defense spending.

This is the most-mouthed campaign promise in Democratic campaign history, and as empty as a politician's heart. Obama knows as much.

No one will argue that there isn't excess in the Department of Defense budget. There are programs that didn't bear fruit, armored systems that were better left on the drawing board, planes that looked good at the time but proved too costly to build, high-tech ships that had potential, but after all the bills were paid to develop them, simply fell short of expectations. In every Pentagon budget there are big-ticket items that, in hindsight, make you wonder who the heck thought that one up – and why on Earth did the Congress put money up for it?

But can anyone truly believe that a man who has no previous hands-on experience with the military, who has never worn the uniform of the U.S. military, who has never spent time with the men and women of our armed forces—on the ground, in the air, or on ships at sea—who does not sit on any one of the major defense authorizing or appropriating committees, can have the chutzpa to claim that he will identify and cut wasteful spending?

There are hundreds of weapon systems that could, under the fast-to-judge, quick-to-cut hand of Obama, be eliminated before they had the chance to prove themselves. If Obama had been in charge when the M1A1 Abrams Main Battle Tank was under development, and a huge financial problem for the military, Obama would have cut it. But its developers persisted, and dollars that might have been considered "waste" by Obama, were spent until the M1A1 became the most lethal, most respected, most effective tank on the battlefield.

Ask any Abrams crewmember who's survived direct hits by high explosive shells and rocket-propelled grenades if he would have cancelled the Abrams and the answer will be a resounding *"No!"*

The list of expensive weapons systems is long: Billion-dollar bombers like the B2; multi-billion dollar ships like the Ford class; billion dollar space-based surveillance systems. At the individual soldier's level, there are new technologies being applied to personal protection; better combat performance; wider-range communications; over-the-horizon information gathering; improved detection and disarming of improvised explosive devices; the list goes on.

Where would Obama make his "cuts"?

Maybe he thinks that spending on military family services is wasteful; maybe he doesn't care for commissaries or post exchanges, where airmen, soldiers, Marines, sailors and Coast Guardsmen stretch their limited incomes to buy the basics for their families. Never mind the facts of protecting our homeland; Obama's budget cutting knife will slash right through the very foundations of our military strength.

**Item 3:  I will cut investments in unproven missile defense systems.**

Once again, Obama's perfect future vision enables him to scrap missile defense programs, even as our nation's enemies prepare very nasty projectiles to hurtle across continents and oceans. On this point, bluntness is in order:

North Korea is going to perfect a long-range missile; Iran is going to perfect their nuclear capability; China and Russia are going to be cheering them on, allying with them and even supplying nuclear warhead delivery systems when it serves their geopolitical interests. To dismiss this thinking as overly reactionary is to dismiss the last 100,000 years of fighting that has gone on among men, uninterrupted. It's a sad truth of the human condition, but a realistic one—which is why we take our selection of a President so seriously.

And in this time of global crisis, to dismiss this thinking is to stupidly open the door to the destruction of our cities and our way of life.

Cutting investments on unproven missile systems is like telling a cotton farmer we're cutting investments in pesticides for future strains of boll weevil. So no worries, Mr. Farmer, about the current boll weevil. But when new strains come along, "Oh well, having some of your cotton is a good thing," Obama would say, while the rest of the crop disintegrates.

"Oh well, having some of our cities is a good thing," Obama would say as Seattle and San Francisco smolder under nuclear clouds.

This philosophy will go over especially well in Israel, as they survey the ruins of Jerusalem and Tel Aviv.

## Item 4: I will not weaponize space.

This one is simple. Someone else will weaponize space. Every nation currently capable of putting a satellite in orbit is also trying to leverage that technology to their own political advantage. Nations on the cusp of developing that technology are salivating over the possibilities of holding a megaton hammer over our heads.

Imagine North Korea's Kim Jong-Il dreaming of a future where his very own orbiting nuke, painted pink to match his fingernails, sails over the United States every 90 minutes.

China would gloat over a geosynchronous armed satellite poised directly over the Western Hemisphere.

The nuclear technology transfers among North Korea, Iran, and China are coalescing into a perfect storm front of space-platform blackmail that will, if left unchecked by a United States President in denial, sweep over our horizon with terrifying consequences.

The high ground in space will belong to the first nation that can hold its position against all comers. If a President Obama would not seize the most advantageous orbital positions and thwart the plans of potential aggressors, there would be no subsequent opportunity to retake the summit.

## Item 5: I will slow our development of future combat systems.

On the sixth anniversary of 9/11, the Obama media machine delivered a message to the America people. It was typically stirring, and reflected the sadness as well as the resolve we all experience when we consider that terrible day. But one paragraph of that message is going to haunt Obama:

> *Our calling today remains the same as it was on 9/11. We must write a new chapter in American history. We must bring justice to the terrorists who killed on our shores. We must devise new strategies, develop new capabilities, and build new alliances to defeat the threats of the 21st century.*[105]

These words of Obama's that *"we must devise new strategies, develop new capabilities"* were delivered just five months before his TV ad in which be promised to *"slow our development of future combat systems."*

If you detect a contradiction, it gets messier still. In his 2006 book *The Audacity of Hope,* Obama wrote:

> *It's time we acknowledge that a defense budget and force structure built principally around the prospect of World War III makes little strategic sense.*

So how many ways does Obama intend to have his cake? He wants weapons systems development to slow down, but he wants the Defense Department to adopt new strategies and capabilities. He wants us to stop planning for WWIII, but he doesn't want to give soldiers new weapons suited to the new urban warfare.

Where has Obama been for the past decade? Certainly not touring our nation's military training centers where the concept of fighting WWIII was discarded some time ago to make way for learning how to fight door-to-door, how to deploy remotely piloted vehicles at the far end of a city, or target in a GPS-guided "smart" bomb 50 miles away.

Is it important to maintain a strategic force to assure our national security from halfway around the globe? Sure. As long as there are enemies capable of doing us harm from more than an arms-length away, we need to be able to respond. But from his own words it appears that Obama equates strategic force with Armageddon, and that's not the real world of the 21st century battlefield. Our men and women in uniform are taking on our enemies on their home turf. We are training our troops to fight wherever, whenever, the enemy emerges. Tactical warfare is every bit as important as our ability to react to an incoming thermonuclear strike from North Korea.

Once again, Obama's naiveté is glaring.

## Item 6: And I will institute an independent defense review board to ensure that the Quadrennial Defense Review [QDR] is not used to justify unnecessary spending.

Obama raises the arcane Quadrennial Defense Review to the level of campaign politics in hopes of sounding all grown up. You know, right after we do the wave and chant *"Yes we can!"* we'll dig into that QDR. And by suggesting that he'll have someone review the people who do the reviewing, Obama positions himself as the citizen cavalry riding into Washington to root out waste, fraud and abuse.

But who's going to review the reviewers of the reviewers?

Seriously, Obama is correct that the QDR can help control spending at the Pentagon, which has a long history of waste. We agree with Obama that watchdogs should keep the Pentagon check-writers in check. They should be scrutinized as fiercely as the next government department. But the Pentagon doesn't need more bureaucratic layers, it needs genuine leadership.

## Item 7: I will set a goal of a world without nuclear weapons.

Obama's running for President but acting like it's the Miss America Contest, *"And I wish for world peace!"*

Obama would have us believe that he can single-handedly convince Pakistan, India, China, Russia, North Korea, Great Britain, France, and Israel to scrap their nuclear arsenals! This isn't just a pipe dream, it smacks of grandiose assumptions of Presidential influence that have no precedent in American or global history (even James Monroe could, at best, only influence the Western Hemisphere).

The nuclear club, whether Obama likes it or not, is comprised of sovereign nations that feel the need to protect their front and back doors with the best possible weapons. There is an old saying Obama should remember from his community organizing days in South Chicago: *You don't bring a knife to a gunfight.* World leaders know this. In 2006, French President Jacques Chirac made it clear that France would retaliate with nukes against any terrorist act involving a nuclear weapon. That is France's right, and if Obama thinks Chirac, or now Nicolas Sarcozy, will listen to his entreaties simply because "he's not Bush" then he's in for a rude awakening.

With so many bad guys working on dirty bombs or trying to steal nukes for even bigger bangs, what peace-loving nation would scrap its own nuclear capabilities just because the new U.S. President asked "pretty please" without any alternative (remember, Barack also wants to trash anti-missile systems)?

Great Britain, France, and Israel, long our allies, don't deserve to be unnerved by a Presidential candidate who lacks the resolve to stand against the terrorists of today or tomorrow.

### Item 8: ...I will not develop new nuclear weapons.

Our nation's nuclear stockpile is aging. Key components from triggers to fissile materials are deteriorating. You can wish that reality away all you want, but it's still reality. And we cannot meet our national defense obligation, or our mutual defense contracts with our allies, by pretending that we don't need to explore new nuclear weapons development. How many times must it be said that terrorists and the nations that sponsor them are pressing forward in their quest to develop nuclear weapons?

Telling the American voters that you will rid the world of nuclear weapons, and also not pursue reasonable alternatives, only serves the interests of our enemies.

**Items 9 & 10: I will seek a global ban on the production of fissile material. I will negotiate with Russia to take our ICBMs off hair-trigger alert and to achieve deep cuts in our nuclear program.**

So Obama would again tell the world that they cannot produce the materials required to create a nuclear chain reaction. *"No fissile materials!"* isn't quite the audience pleaser as *"Yes we can!"* but it's an equally vapid pledge. Nations that have established nuclear programs must maintain them by replacing aging fissile materials and assuring long-term viability of their defensive systems.

There is little chance that China, North Korea, Iran, or Russia will ever move away from fissile materials production. Even if they pledged to do so, any astute observer of the history of international agreements would know that at least one of the signatories was lying.

This leads into promise #10 to negotiate with Russia to take our intercontinental ballistic missiles off "hair trigger" alert and achieve deep cuts in our nuclear program. Once again, this is a promise born of ignorance. Does Obama really believe that the men and women who man our nuclear weapons are in Cold War mode, sitting in their Dr. Strangelovian cocoons, fingers poised over the launch buttons, ready at a moment's notice to unleash World War III?

The only accurate part of this scenario is the "moments notice" part, but that does not equate to "hair trigger."

Arms limitation negotiations between the United States and Russia have been on-going since Obama was running kites in Indonesia. Many Presidents have come and gone since

SALT I, SALT II, and START, and the numbers of missiles and war-heads our two countries have is half of what it was in 1990, and steadily dropping. Each of the superpowers has, essentially, cut off one testicle. The odds of removing the second one are slim. Obama's arrival in Moscow with a scalpel will not go over well. Russian leader Dmitry Medvedev would say to Obama, *"You do the work on yourself first, then we'll see."*

Russia certainly isn't going to agree to deeper strategic cuts in an era when their oil fields are pumping gold, a restless China is sitting on the border eying Russia's newfound glory, and terror-ists rim the southern borders eager to sabotage Russia's economic growth.

Which brings us back to the USS Ford. An Obama presi-dency, in its seventh year, may very well find itself in need of some serious weaponry and manpower to beat back a new enemy we face then. It may be an enemy well-versed in urban warfare, sponsored by a major power whose assets include seaborne and airborne weapons systems, possibly even space-based weapons. President Obama will go to his cupboard of national security and discover that it is bare – emptied by his fulfilled campaign promis-es. At 3 a.m., when the Secretary of Defense calls, Obama could have nothing left to offer, and the seven years we will need to repair the damage will be an eternity in the life of our Republic.

# Making up foreign policy on the fly.

*The notion that somehow not talking to countries is punishment to them…is ridiculous*
*(July 23, 2007)*

*"We need to talk to Iran and Syria"*
*(February 3, 2008)*

*I trust the American people to understand that it's not weakness, but wisdom to talk not just to our friends, but our enemies – like Roosevelt did, and Kennedy did, and Truman did*[106]
*(May 9, 2008)*

*After eight years of the disastrous policies of George Bush,
it is time to pursue direct diplomacy, with friend and
foe alike, without preconditions* [107]
*(May 22, 2008)*

*I would meet with our adversaries, including Iran,
including Venezuela, including Cuba,
including North Korea, without preconditions* [108]
*(May 04, 2008)*

**Our world is full of evil, lunatic despots salivating at the opportunity to kill Americans and bring down our nation – Iran's Mahmoud Ahmadinejad, Syria's Bashar al-Assad, Venezuela's Hugo Chavez, North Korea's Kim Jong-Il, al-Qaeda's Osama bin Laden, Sudan's Hassan al-Bashir, Zimbabwe's Robert Mugabe, Burma's ruling junta.**

**A President Obama would be a very busy man in his freshman year, having promised on numerous occasions to hold direct talks with any one of our enemies at any time without precondition.**

Obama wants us to think that George Bush's refusal to meet with our enemies is not only *"ridiculous"* but *"a disgrace."* Or at least that's what the rookie Senator from Illinois said until adult supervision was brought in.

## I will always talk to our enemies, or not.

From the outset of his campaign for President, Obama insisted that he would engage our enemies while those cowboy Republicans oppose engagement. The far left loved hearing him trash Bush, so whatever else he said was fine by them. Obama was the long-awaited "unifier" in their eyes, so any divisive comments he might make were irrelevant.

But of course, nothing is more relevant than a President's approach to national security affairs. Nothing. Obama understands this in the way that a schoolboy might, but not in the way a seasoned statesman might.

That's why Obama cited Franklin Roosevelt and Harry Truman as Presidents who met with enemies. But maybe he skipped 10th grade history where they (used to) teach that neither Roosevelt nor Truman ever met with Axis leaders. Roosevelt did meet with Soviet dictator Stalin at Yalta, and Truman met with Stalin at Potsdam, but Stalin was a wartime ally.

Then as the war turned cold, Truman no longer met with Stalin. Or China's dictator Mao. Or North Korea's dictator Kim Il Sung. Truman was alert during those 10th grade history classes while Obama was, as he writes in his memoirs, often out smoking dope.

Truman understood the incredible damage that the naïve appeasing diplomats of 1930s Europe caused. As former UN Ambassador John Bolton has written:

> *While the diplomats of European democracies played with their umbrellas, the Nazis were rearming and expanding their industrial power. In today's world of weapons of mass destruction, time is again a precious asset, one almost invariably on the side of the would-be proliferators. Time allows them to perfect the complex science and technology necessary to sustain nuclear weapons and missile programs, and provides far greater opportunity for concealing their activities from our ability to detect and, if necessary, destroy them.*[109]

Once he began taking flak for this frighteningly naïve position, Obama had a chance to plead ignorance and go back to re-read those 10th grade history books. Instead, he dug himself deeper in.

He next cited John Kennedy's meeting with Nikita Khrushchev as an example to emulate. Again, he could not have pinned the tail further from the donkey. Kennedy was young and untested—in that the comparison to Obama holds.  But when Kennedy did meet with Khrushchev and the Soviet leader took a measure of the man, all hell broke lose and our nation was hurtled in the months that followed into the most dangerous crisis of the nuclear age.

Going in, Kennedy was well aware of the risks he was taking.  His Harvard thesis had been titled "Appeasement at Munich."  Senior advisor George Kennan had strenuously argued against rushing into a high-level meeting, arguing that Khrushchev would turn the affair into anti-American propaganda. Kennedy's Secretary of State Dean Rusk also tried to stop his boss, asking in a *Foreign Affairs* article:

> *Is it wise to gamble so heavily? Are not these two men who should be kept apart until others have found a sure meeting ground of accommodation between them?*

But Kennedy was young and obstinate, like Obama. He went ahead and met Khrushchev with no preconditions. And he got a hard lesson in realpolitic—Khrushchev wasn't interested in finding common ground or a path toward peace, only in weakening and exploiting his rival. That's how evil works.

Obama would have been wiser to cite the case of Richard Nixon who met with the Chinese—but only because Nixon had a card to play. If Obama were to read Henry Kissinger's book, *The White House Years*, he would learn of the hundreds of meetings over 18 months between lower-level diplomats from the U.S. and China before Nixon and Chairman Mao met in January 1970 in Warsaw.  Obama would learn of Kissinger's secret visit to Beijing to hammer on the Chinese.  And most importantly, he would learn that the Chinese didn't change because of a Presidential visit.  As Kissinger later wrote:

> *China was induced to rejoin the community of nations less by the prospect of dialogue with the United States*

*than by fear of being attacked by its ostensible ally, the Soviet Union.*

Nixon was instrumental in transforming the world's largest and most deadly totalitarian dictatorship because he convinced Mao that it was in his best interests to change, not because of a meet-and-greet in Warsaw.

Obama would have been equally wise to cite the case of Ronald Reagan who refused to meet with the Soviets until after the arms race exposed the Soviet economy for a centrally planned sham. Reagan rebuilt the U.S. military, restored confidence in American intentions, and pressured the Soviets with the specter of a missile defense shield. Having done all this, Reagan was then in the position to attend a summit meeting holding all the cards.

Obama could also have cited the case of George Bush who used the fear of American resolve after 9/11 to pressure Muammar al-Gaddafi of Libya to surrender his chemical, biological and nuclear weapons programs. And a good thing, for we found soon thereafter that Libya's military programs were more advanced than CIA intel had thought.

Instead of citing a relevant case of diplomacy, Obama played the fool. Then his handlers stepped in. They told him, in no uncertain terms, no doubt, that he was coming across as a rank amateur, and further, that if he ever intended to get into the Oval Office other than as part of a tour group, he'd better admit to being ignorant or throw some fancy head-and-shoulder fakes. He chose the latter.

He insisted that his speeches had been *misinterpreted*. And that he had, in fact, always intended to meet with the global bad boys *only after* his staff had fully prepared for the meetings.

Of course, he was as transparent as cellophane. And in choosing the head fake, he opened himself up to the fair question:

What would you *really* do once in office, Mr. Obama?

One can easily imagine a rookie President Obama, bound and determined to prove the grandness of his intellect, meeting with Iran's Mahmoud Ahmadinejad in some neutral location, such as Caracas. His own wife Michelle has spoke of his obstinacy, as we noted earlier:

> He seems to have a fact about everything. He can argue and debate about anything. It doesn't matter if he agrees with you, he can still argue with you. Sometimes, he's even right.[110]

Maybe a meeting in Caracas could be a two-fer for the high-achieving Obama. He could also convince Venezuelan madman Hugo Chavez to stop undermining democracies throughout the Americas. Or maybe Obama would focus on one madman at a time.

**Obama's meeting with Ahmadinejad would make for a great photo opportunity—two men of Muslim heritage, posing together on the world stage. With the whole world watching the two leaders on their TVs, the reactions would be immediate and telling.**

Iranians would feel proud of their leader who is facing Presidential elections in 2009 and could use a summit with Obama as proof of his enhanced stature. Ahmadinejad would surely tell his people that talks with Washington came as a direct result of his hard-line agenda. And what agenda is that? To wipe the "filthy bacteria" of Israel off the map with the help of terrorist proxies Hamas and Hezbollah, then finish developing nuclear weapons to dominate the Middle East and, eventually perhaps, the world. At least that's what Ahmadinejad has said publicly. That's how evil works.

Other nations would greet the end of the mullahs' isolation by rushing to Tehran armed with business deals, oil contracts, diplomatic agreements—all undermining the very sanctions and isolation that Obama has said he would employ against Iran.

Iran has shown that they will act in this manner. After five years of negotiations with the Europeans, the only result is that Iran is five years closer to having nuclear weapons. (North Korea has used similar summit talks to gain the time they needed to complete testing of a nuclear weapon in 2006.)

And what does Obama think he can offer Ahmadinejad to convince him to act like more of a gentleman? Iran's top military goal is an immediate U.S. withdrawal from Iraq. That is also Obama's goal. So why should Iran alter its behavior if Obama gives them what they want, without preconditions?

As seasoned diplomats know, the biggest tactical risk of holding a summit with adversary heads of state is that it creates tremendous pressure for "results." Both sides want to announce to the folks back home that they have wrestled concessions out of their opponent. So in holding a summit, the conditions and concessions need to be hammered out in advance. What concessions does Obama imagine Ahmadinejad will make to him on Iran's nuclear program? And what new concessions will Obama offer?

Toss Lebanon to Syria's butchers?

Take Hamas off the terrorist list?

Put the screws to Israel?

All items on Ahmadinejad's agenda, but how about on Obama's agenda?

If Obama genuinely believes he can change Iran's behavior by meeting with Ahmadinejad without preconditions, he should tell the American people what his plans are, and tell us in specific terms, before the election. If Obama does not give an explanation, voters may wonder if he has some secret plan up his sleeve. Voters may also wonder if Obama is utterly out of his depth on national security.

## I will never use nuclear weapons, or not.

Once a politician as young and athletic as Obama begins throwing head-and-shoulder fakes, things can get real blurry—for everyone. He had been clear for months that nuclear weapons were "off the table" in any conflict between the U.S. and Iran. Then, when pressed, he shifted hard right and stated firmly that he would use all means necessary to defend our nation.  Which is it?

Listening to Obama, you get the impression he can go both ways in a political scrimmage.  One day he's playing offense and his instincts are to run a student body left formation; but the next day he's on defense countering his own arguments.  Playing both ways is fine at the high school level, but not in the pros.  It's too easy to get, and cause, hurt.  Obama's  movements are so swift and slippery that political consultant Karl Rove has commented:

> *Is Mr. Obama's first instinct to dismiss North Korea, the world's worst nuclear proliferator, as an insignificant threat?  Is his immediate reaction to treat Venezuela as a wayward child, rather than as an adversary willing to destabilize the hemisphere?  Is his memory so short he has forgotten the Castro brothers' willingness to aid revolutionary movements?  Is he so shortsighted as to ignore the threat to Mideast stability that Syria's meddling in Lebanon and support for Hamas and Hezbollah represents?[111]*

Good questions, all.  Will we get answers in time?

# I will pull all troops out of Iraq, or not.

As with the "any thug, any time" policy and the "no nukes, not no nukes" policy, Obama's positions on Iraq have turned him into a whirling dervish on the political court.

**"All troops out immediately"**
**"All troops out on a timetable"**
**"Some troops out, slowly"**

Where does Obama really stand? What will he tell the young National Guardsmen and women, or the seasoned Reservists who are wondering if they will ever see home again for more than a few weeks? If he's so wishy-washy about their service that he can't decide to bring them home or keep them deployed, what are they to think? Under this kind of yes-you-can-no-you-can't leadership, 1600 Pennsylvania Avenue becomes just another Waffle House.

Is he simply so young and inexperienced that his opinions on the weighty issues are unformed, and still evolving? Or is he by default a natural contrarian, delighting in the give and take of political discourse, energized by the wordplay and the possibilities, not beholden to any particular point of view and capable of debating either side with equal ardor?

Neither explanation comforts us.

What we know for certain is the theme of Obama's candidacy: statement/retraction. We have a man on a playground seesaw. The man is straddling the middle, giving himself a ride, alternately tipping left, then right, with the issue of our national security appearing to be little more than a distraction.

To the men and women on the front lines, and those patrolling our waters, our airspace, and our still-too-porous borders, the war on terror is no playground ride; it is the deadly serious business of protecting the homeland of their families and their communities – still at risk of a madman's inglorious plans.

Until Obama is ready to take a position he can defend without equivocating, he is only amusing himself, while those who lie in wait to hurt us harbor almost unbridled hope that he will be elected.

## Why are so many terrorists heaping praises on Obama?

*We like Mr. Obama—*
*we hope he will [win] the election*
--Ahmed Yousef, leader of Hamas

*After studying Obama's electro campaign manifes-*
*to I thought this is a man that's capable of change*
Volunteer at a Palestinian phonebank calling
American voters urging support of Obama

*Obama's the best choice because he's
"less tied" to the Cold War*
--Gleb Pavlovsky, Russian architect
of a new Cold War

*[Effectively endorsing Obama by
calling McCain] a man of war.*
Hugo Chávez, anti-American
President of Venezuela

*[Effectively endorsing Obama by claiming in a fic-
tional TV show that] McCain is orchestrating numerous conspiracies against the Islamic Republic.*
Iran Intelligence Ministry

*[Endorsing Obama by accusing McCain and others
for trying to mount] a base and ridiculous challenge
[to North Korea as part of] a bid to strangle it.*
North Korea newspaper, *Rodong Sinmun*

*Obama is a good man, and kindhearted
Shaaban Abdel Rahim, Lebanese musician known*
for *"I Hate Israel"* and "Hey People, It Was Only a
Tower"

We suspect that Obama hasn't welcomed all the fan mail
he's received from the enemies of America. We also suspect he's
worked hard to hush up some of his more radical supporters, at
least until after the election. But what does it say when people
who are the sworn enemies of the State, people who have been
actively killing our soldiers, endorse a Presidential candidate even
indirectly?

We know that Ronald Reagan was furious to learn that
the Ku Klux Klan had endorsed his candidacy. Reagan was no

friend of the Klan's hateful past which was more associated with Southern Democratic politics, anyway. So is it fair to tar Obama with the hate of America's enemies? No, and yes.

No, because Obama is a decent young man.

Yes, because there are at least eight things Obama would do as President that would delight our enemies, and that's why they are endorsing him. Let's review:

## 1. Would yank troops out of Iraq.

When Obama votes to de-authorize funding for our troops in Iraq, it sends one message to our soldiers ("all your sacrifice has been in vain"), another to our allies ("can't count on the U.S. in a pinch"), and still another to our enemies ("you can tear up the middle east all you want now; we'll look the other way").

## 2. Would not listen in on terrorists' calls.

Since 9/11 our counterterrorism forces have tracked down sleeper cell operatives in the U.S. who were reporting to al-Qaeda's #2 man, Khalid Sheik Mohammed; we've foiled an attempt to blow up the Brooklyn Bridge and kill thousands; we've stopped Mohammed Babar who was planning to blow up half of downtown London. We shut these terrorists down—largely because of the Patriot Act and aggressive surveillance activity.

But Obama would have none of this. He has been a vocal opponent of warrantless wiretapping with a September 10 mindset and a remarkable ignorance on the subject, especially for someone who has taught constitutional law at the University of Chicago. In an interview with ABC News, Obama argued his case:

> We can crack down on threats against the United States, but we can do so within the constraints of our Constitution...what we know is that, in previous terrorist attacks—for example, the first attack against

*the World Trade Center—we were able to arrest those responsible, put them on trial.*

Obama is here embracing the approach of the 1990s that Bill Clinton insisted upon, and thus shows a remarkable blindness to the reason we have been safe since 9/11: the Bush Administration's efforts to move from "prosecuting criminals" to "protecting against terrorists."

Because Clinton treated the 1993 World Trade Center bombing as simply a crime, our investigation was a slow, tedious affair. So slow that we didn't figure out that bin Laden was responsible for four long years.  And we know what happened during those years: bin Laden dug himself deeper and deeper into an impregnable network of caves in Afghanistan while his al-Qaeda soldiers attacked the United States over and over with impunity.

But after 9/11, the approach to fighting terrorists changed. Our forces were allowed to go on the offensive—still operating within the bounds of the Constitution, no matter how hard Obama tries to argue otherwise. (Protections in the Fourth, Fifth and Sixth Amendments relating to prosecution under criminal law are not relevant.  Intelligence activities that do not lead to prosecution are not covered.) Most importantly, there have been no attacks on native soil.

But Obama would require our counterterror investigations to once again be conducted within a law enforcement framework. What does that mean?

Let's say a suspected terrorist places a phone call to a fellow terrorist to launch an attack.  We won't be able to legally tap that call under a President Obama, because the terrorists' civil liberties are again more important than national security.

Just like they were on September *10th*.

Terrorists can't believe their good fortune.

### 3. Would take no action against sleeper cells on U.S. soil.

Ali Saleh Kahlah al-Marri is a U.S. resident being held in a South Carolina military brig. He is an al-Qaeda sleeper agent who moved into the U.S. on September 10, 2001, so as to arouse no suspicion. When he was caught, al-Marri, a capable engineer, was preparing to unleash deadly cyanide on the public, and to wreak havoc with the U.S. banking system.

Bush Administration lawyers want to keep al-Marri locked up indefinitely. Defense counsel counters that "as long as the President can detain *anyone* he wants, *nobody* is safe." (Note to counsel: Your client is the *only* such sleeper agent being so detained.)

This is a legal case headed for the Supreme Court. So it bears consideration:

Would Obama's judicial appointments support a nation's right to safety over a terrorist's right to due process? We believe the latter would occur under Obama. And we wonder how many more sleeper agents, on native soil, still await their orders.

### 4. Would encourage decent Muslims to turn a deaf ear.

We are told that Islam is a religion of peace. We are told that the vast majority of Muslim people are good-hearted people. So what are we missing?

Do good-hearted people sit silently by while their radical brothers commit horrific acts of violence in the name of their religion?

Would good-hearted people attending the annual convention of the Islamic Society of North America in Chicago in September 2006 give these kinds of answers to polling questions:

- Is the American government at war with the religion of Islam? **68% said yes.**

- Did Muslims hijack planes and fly them into buildings on 9/11? **45% said no.**

- Was the U.S. invasion of Afghanistan after 9/11 justified?

- **81% said no.**[112]

We don't get it.  We wonder why these good-hearted Muslims aren't first to the frontlines in the fight against their radical brothers.  Or why they don't organize a Million Muslim March on Washington to demand an end to Muslim hate and intolerance.

To the contrary, we expect to see quite the opposite in an Obama Administration.  **These good-hearted Muslims could, with the help of Obama-appointed judges, demand special privileges uniquely their own as detailed in some obscure passage of the Quran.**

What politically correct liberal could refuse the requests of the long-oppressed Muslims in their struggle for special privileges?

Certainly not Obama.

## 5. Would continue liberal tradition of trashing the troops.

As liberals go, Obama is fairly solicitous of our fighting men and women.  Only once in the primary campaign did he slip and say something unguarded, something causing people to wonder what he really thinks:

> **We've got to get the job done there [in Afghanistan] and that requires us to have enough troops so that we're not just air-raiding villages and killing civilians, which is causing enormous pressure over there.**[113]

**So far in the campaign, Obama has been forgiven this accusation, though we don't really understand why.** It is wrong on all counts. And it reminds us of a similar accusation another liberal Senator made once about the conduct of our U.S. military:

...they had personally raped, cut off ears, cut off heads, taped wires from portable telephones to human genitals and turned up the power, cut off limbs, blown up bodies, randomly shot at civilians, razed villages in fashion reminiscent of Genghis Khan, shot cattle and dogs for fun, poisoned food stocks, and generally ravaged the countryside of South Vietnam...

This was John Kerry speaking about Vietnam. When he made these anti-military comments in 1971, just as when Obama makes his own anti-military comments now, our enemies figure we must be weak and divided, so they redouble their efforts against us. It also gives them ideas about what will inflame U.S. public opinion, so they learn quickly how to replicate "horrific" acts and shine the mirror of guilt in our direction.

When we hear our liberal politicians slandering and maliciously skewering our troops, we assume it is for their own selfish agenda—that is, to get elected at any price.

Neither what our enemies are hearing, or what we're hearing, is a recommendation for Obama.

## 6. Would make racial profiling even sillier.

Right now we have liberals insisting on racial profiling in just about every walk of life...except where it matters.

They want just the right number of blacks at Harvard, just the right number of women in the executive suite, just enough set-asides for Native Americans. But in the one place where we need the most sophisticated racial profiling systems we can build—that is, in airport security screening, liberals make more noise than two donkeys having a kicking match in a tin barn.

So with Obama proudly towing the ACLU-vetted line on this, expect that the only official opposition to profiling will be when our national security is on the line.

And if there is another attack involving airplanes, expect the Obama media machine to blame Bush for not catching the terrorists on his watch. This mindless approach to our national security is insanely dangerous. It is foolishness to allow the PC lunacy that forces long lines at the airport while 85-year-old great grandfathers and "the Golden Girls" get shaken down.

We need to shake down young Arab men. They fit the profile. They should be scrutinized until our intel tells us otherwise. No apologies to the PC crowd. It's Arabs, young ones, mostly men. Put them through the ringer.

## 7. Would react rather clumsily to nuclear attack.

How would Obama react to a nuclear attack? Here's what he said at the Democratic debate in April 2007:

> Well, first thing we'd have to do is make sure that we've got an effective emergency response. The second thing is to make sure we've got good intelligence, A, to find out that we don't have other threats and attacks potentially out there, and B, to find out do we have any intelligence on who might have carried it out so that we can take potentially some action to dismantle that network.

Apparently, Obama believes in watching the horse run out of the burning barn rather than trying to figure out how to keep the barn from burning down in the first place. The national security solution, lost on Obama, is to strengthen our intelligence agencies and give them the tools they need to seek out and destroy terrorist networks (not to *"take potentially some action,"* whatever that means). Is this the intellectual rigor Obama's fans rave about? It certainly wouldn't pass muster in a class taught by another black man, Thomas Sowell, who brings a distinguished perspective to his every teaching, and has concluded thusly about Obama:

> There is no reason why someone as arrogant, foolishly clever and ultimately dangerous as Barack Obama should become President, especially not at a time when the

*threat of international terrorists with nuclear weapons looms over 300 million Americans.*[114]

## 8. Would legitimize brutal dictators worldwide

Much has been made of Obama's willingness to meet with any thug, any time – legitimizing them in their own countries and around the globe. But interestingly, Obama is reported to have told his handlers that he "just didn't understand" why he was taking so much flack for wanting to meet with our enemies.

Is he that lacking in imagination? That historically naïve? That cut-off from realities outside his narrow view of the world? These are certainly the questions our enemies are asking.

# Forsaking honesty for the presidency.

Honesty has a name. It is Thane Rosenbaum who wrote in May 2008 that he had voted against George Bush—twice. A human-rights law professor; the events at Abu Ghraib and Guantanamo Bay, as well as the Patriot Act and wiretapping, trouble him deeply. But as a New York City resident, he was there for the 9/11 carnage and he recalls quite vividly how on 9/12 in New York and in cities across America we expected another terrorist strike any moment; the stock market collapsed on such fears; we grew to hate air travel; sarin and anthrax entered our national vocabulary as did orange and yellow threat codes; we all waited for terrorism's second shoe to drop, and, seven years later ... no shoe. Cities around the world have been hit, with massive losses of lives. But America has been safe from suicide bombers, biological warfare, and collapsing skyscrapers. Still, George Bush is regularly ridiculed and labeled the worst President in American history. When an enemy succeeds as al-Qaeda did, and then seven years pass without an incident, there are two reasonable conclusions: Either they've taken a long breather, or they've been thwarted.

**Thane Rosenbaum asks in all honesty if George Bush is the reason we are safe today?** [115]

**Would that Obama speak so honestly.** Few would put George Bush's presidency up on a pedestal. But when Obama insists that somehow we are unsafe because of Bush, or when his supporters portray Bush as evil incarnate and Obama greedily fans the flames, we are seeing an extraordinarily ambitious man who will say or do anything to gain power. As his best friend Valerie Jarrett says, *"He's always wanted to be President."* So in his drive to the Oval Office, has he become the very model of the modern petty politician?

# 13. Misguided Tax Policies Stunting The USA?

> *He gains votes ever and anew by taking*
> *money from everybody and giving it to a few,*
> *while explaining that every penny was extracted*
> *from the few to be giving to the many.*
> *—Ogden Nash*

In this poem about a politician of 60 years ago, Ogden Nash might have had Obama in mind. For few politicians have worn the mask of Robin Hood with greater ease, pretending to be taking from the rich when in fact his tax policies would take from rich and poor alike.

## Obama wears the mask of Robin Hood...sideways.

Obama threw down the gauntlet to all the king's men and intensified a divisive class war, pitting rich against poor with this passage in *The Audacity of Hope*:

> The rich in America have little to complain about. Between 1971 and 2001, while the median wage and salary income of the average worker showed literally no gain, the income of the top hundredth of a percent went up almost 500 percent. The distribution of wealth is even more skewed, and levels of inequality are now higher than at any time since the Gilded Age.

From the mouth of Reverend Wright, such overexcited rhetoric could be expected. But from his acolyte Obama?

Obama is correct in saying that a few enterprising souls have grown very rich as a result of our transition to an "information" era, just as a few made fortunes in an earlier transition to the "industrial" area, also known as the Gilded Age.  But he's playing fast and loose with relevance here.  He accuses the *"top hundredth of a percent"* of making too much money, 500% too much apparently.

So how many of us Americans are actually included in Obama's *"top hundredth of a percent"*?  Figuring there are roughly 200 million Americans of working age, Obama is referring to 20,000 of us. Just 20,000 people in a big nation with a $14 trillion economy.

These incredibly bright or fortunate 20,000 are the reason the huddled masses should storm the castle walls and redistribute all the gold to themselves?

## How much higher will Obama raise taxes?

George Bush will go down in history as the biggest spender of all time.  His 2009 budget calls for spending of $3.1 trillion, 55% more than when he took office. Some of that cash was required to bulk up our defense preparedness after 9/11, but most of it was the result of a Republican President using a Democratic goodies-for-votes strategy.

**Our government has long spent money like a drunken sailor; Bush spent like a whole drunken navy.  It's hard to imagine any President spending more than Bush.**

Yet candidate Obama wants to increase already bloating federal spending by another $303 billion—about a 10% increase.[116]  Obama has offered no plans to limit any kind of spending, except on defense—in a time of war, as we've shown, he will slash our vital national security forces.  But beyond that, he wouldn't cut a thing—not the bloated entitlement programs, not the scandalous earmarks, not the socialist farm subsidies.

Obama believes most sincerely that he is obligated to raise taxes in order to pay for all the increased spending he intends.  He is as ignorant on tax policy as he is on defense policy, as we will see.  But he dearly believes it, as does Speaker of the House Nancy Pelosi and Senate Majority Leader Harry Reid—potentially the three most powerful people in Washington in 2009. So the first item on Obama's and the Democrat's tax agenda is to allow the Bush tax cuts to expire. Obama confirmed his intentions on a number of occasions.

In the summer of 2007 at Howard University, Obama said of the Bush tax cuts:

> *People didn't need them, and they weren't even asking for them, and that's why they need to be less, so that we can pay for universal healthcare and other initiatives.*[117]

Six months later in another Democratic debate, Obama was asked if he would let the Bush tax cuts lapse, effectively raising taxes on millions of Americans. He replied:

> *I'm not bashful about it.*[118]

Democrats have been remarkably effective in portraying Bush's tax cuts as the fifth horseman of the financial apocalypse. Republicans have been scramble-brained in their defense of a few tax truths.

In the past four years, income tax cuts have in fact been good for the American economy. Those cuts have raised government tax revenues by $785 billion, and helped create an estimated eight million new jobs and an unprecedented 52 consecutive months of job growth prior to the recession which finally came in 2008.[119]

But these truths aren't being heard on the campaign trail.

We also aren't hearing this important tidbit: the tax revenue that the federal government takes in as a percent of our GDP (gross domestic product) is already very high, by historical standards. In 2007, the figure was 18.8%.[120] This means that when you look at the value of all the goods and services produced in our country, 18.8% of that value was handed over to the federal government. In the past 25 years, this level was only exceeded once, during the second Clinton term. Taxes are already at historically high levels.

Allowing the Bush tax cut to expire, which is what Obama has promised to do, will translate into the largest increase in personal income taxes since World War II.[121] By some estimates, the Obama tax increase would be twice what Lyndon Johnson levied to finance the war in Vietnam and the war on poverty.

But the sad reality potentially facing Obama and Democratic Party leaders is—their jacking of tax rates won't net them much if any more money to spend, as we'll see.

Here is a summary of how the tax pain will be delivered when the tax code changes made in 2001 and 2003 expire (currently scheduled to expire in 2010, unless Obama "cancels the cuts" effective the day he takes office 2009):

- **Marginal tax rates will rise across the board**

- **High income earners will see a 13% increase in tax rates**

- **Some lower-income households will see a 50% increase in tax rates**

- **The marriage penalty will return**

- **The child credit of $500 will go away**

- **Long-term capital gains taxes will rise from 15% to 20%**

- **The top tax rate on dividends will shoot from 15% to 39.6%**

- **The estate tax will return with a top rate of 55% and an exempt amount of only $600,000**

- **The Alternative Minimum Tax will again reach deep into the middle class, ensnaring 25 million tax filers in its web**

The above are not partisan talking points. They are the old tax laws before Bush chiseled away at them. They are the laws we return to automatically when Obama lets the Bush tax cuts expire. Obama's media machine will spit and flay about these numbers, insisting that they are only attacking the "top hundredth of one per-cent" of taxpayers, or only those *"rich CEO bastards"* as Obama's supporters put it. But only the most gullible voters will bite.

Our intelligence tells us that Obama has no intention of waiting until 2010 to get his hands on the tax revenues *he thinks he needs* to fund all the items on his "change" agenda.

## Capital gains taxes are Obama target #1.

Obama is expected to move quickly to repeal the cut in the capital gains tax and take it from 15% back up to 25%, even 28% or 30%. He has labored hard to convince nervous voters that this will not translate into a tax increase for middle-class fami-lies, whom he describes as people with annual incomes lower than $250,000. That may be considered middle-class in the posh neighborhoods Obama inhabits. But that's considered "rich" to most of us.

At a Democratic debate in Philadelphia, Obama vowed to protect middle-class earners:

> *I not only have pledged not to raise their taxes…I've been the first candidate in this race to specifically say I would cut their taxes.* [122]

Obtuse double negatives notwithstanding, an increase in capital gains taxes will affect the 100 million Americans who own stock, including millions of people who fit Mr. Obama's definition of middle class. For the tax year 2005, the IRS tells us that 47% of all households with incomes below $50,000 reported capital gains. And 79% of all tax households with incomes below

$100,000 reported capital gains.  So essentially, the only people unaffected by Obama's proposed capital gains tax hike are the people already unaffected.

At the Philadelphia debate, moderator Charles Gibson pointed out this little discrepancy, which so often goes unmentioned in Mr. Obama's fawning press coverage.

Obama just huffed at Gibson's audacity.

But credit Gibson. He probed even deeper, and asked Obama an even more important question: Why increase the capital gains tax when history proves *higher* rates translate into *lower* revenues?

Having just spent one of his three allowed huffs, Obama next went for the head-fake, and lashed out at greedy robber baron hedge fund managers. It was a predictable feint, and Gibson rolled with it.  He cited government statistics of how tax revenues actually *increased* when capital gains rates had been lowered. Conversely, tax revenues had *decreased* when capital gains rates had been raised.  It's counterintuitive, yes, until you think about it.

When in 2003, George Bush cut the capital gains rate to 15%, investors sold off more of their stocks and assets—to take advantage of the lower tax rates.  Treasury receipts from capital gains increased from $49 billion in 2002 to $110 billion in 2006.

That's one example in time.  Here's another:

In 1986, capital gains taxes were kicked from 20% up to 28% and, as a result, the federal government took in 13% less revenue at the higher 28% rate.[123]

When confronted with hard statistics such as these, Obama used up a second allowed huff and snootily dismissed the whole issue:

> ...*might happen, or it might not. It depends on what's happening on Wall Street and how business is going.*

And eager to be sidetracked, Obama again head-faked into a raging complaint about greedy lenders screwing over homeowners in the sub-prime mortgage crisis. The takeaway?

Either the rookie Senator is ignorant of actual tax theory and revenue data, or he prefers higher tax rates as a matter of principle. Whichever it is, it is not Presidential behavior.

**We suspect that a quick perusal of Obama's home library would find a *Complete Idiot's Guide to Taxes* on the shelf.**

An examination of the Obama family tax returns for 2001 to 2006 revealed some interesting insights into the Obama's tax experience. Ryan Ellis of the American Shareholders Association did the study, and he found that the couple reported only $1,188 in dividends in 2006, $2,754 in dividends in 2005, and none previous to that. Even though Michelle Obama was paid over $1 million from the University of Chicago's Hospital System during this time, she has never opened a 401(k) plan or IRA. So maybe Obama is comfortable raiding our investment earnings because he doesn't understand the whole "invest for your future" thing. He is young, after all. He doesn't, as Mr. Ellis puts it, *"have any skin in the game."*[124]

## What will our new tax bills add up to?

**When all of Obama's expected tax hikes are tallied up – the end to the Bush tax cut, a raise in the income tax rate, higher tax on capital gains, a higher ceiling on Social Security taxes, along with an increase in payroll taxes – a family making $200,000 a year can count on coughing up $30,000 as the price of an Obama presidency.**

## Ignoring the facts that don't support his socialist dreams.

Obama sees a government capable of vastly expanding its programs in the areas of healthcare, education, nutrition, and children. As a rather dogmatic politician, Obama has a clear idea of what he wants.  Indeed those close to him say he feels a certain calling, an almost messianic belief that he knows what's right for us all.  He believes his commitment to minorities and the poor exalts him in the political animal kingdom. He believes that those who oppose him are simply deficient in brainpower, and that he can bring oppose him are simply deficient in brainpower, and that he can win them over through the force of his intellect. In his book Obama writes:

> I admire many Americans of great wealth and don't begrudge their success in the least. I know that many if not most have earned it through hard work, building businesses and creating jobs and providing value to their customers. I simply believe that those of us who have benefited most from this new economy…can afford to pay a bit more in taxes.[125]

By including himself in the group of people *"who have benefited most from this new economy,"* **Obama opens the door to three interesting observations:**

1. People *have* benefited; so the Bush economic policies are not the failures he claims.

2. People who word hard should be *penalized* so people who don't work can be *rewarded.*

3. There are two Americas—the "makers" and the "takers" and what's needed is a "raker" to even things out.

This last point, about there being "two Americas," is an essential element of the McGovern-Mondale-Kerry-Obama world view.  Liberals build this into their platforms because they believe it, presumably, and they don't think they can get elected any other way.

In this view, there are two Americas: One is populated with rich white Republicans; the other teeming with the forgotten who hold onto the bottom rungs only with the help of kindhearted Democrats.

That the truth is quite different doesn't matter.

The Census Bureau, which couldn't care less who is partying in the White House, has released some interesting data on the "two Americas" argument.[126] In tracking personal income back to 1967, the Census Bureau stat guys found that the richest 20% of all households generate 50% all income, while the poorest 20% of all households generate 3.4% of all income. This disparity between the richest 20% and poorest 20% has in fact widened over time. It appears to support Obama's argument that the rich are getting richer while the poor are getting poorer.

What's more, the Census Bureau reports that the median household income in 2006 was $48,201, only a few bucks ahead of where it was eight years earlier. This does sound like middle-class stagnation...until you look closer at how demographic changes in America have distorted the statistics and thus the storyline.

The poor's piece of the American pie shrunk from 4.1% in 1970 to 3.4% over 35 years. But the pie itself has grown enormously – our gross domestic product of $14 trillion is three times larger than it was in 1970. When the Census folks factor in the population growth in America, they tell us that the bottom 20% are actually 36% better off today. They sure aren't wealthy, but neither are they poorer. A rising tide has—*gasp!*—lifted all boats.

Middle class households have also been misrepresented by Obama because of the changing face of America. Since 1970 there has been a dramatic rise in divorced, never-married and single-person households. Back in 1970, nearly three-fourths of all households fit the Ozzie and Harriet mold. Today, only half do. In 1970 there were 3.14 people in each house, today there are 2.57. Since our incomes are measured by household and not by person, the middle-class household in America actually enjoys a higher standard of living today.

This is not to excuse or wish away the problems of the U.S. economy, only to lend perspective. **When Obama paints a picture of two America's, if you listen close enough you can almost hear him say there's the masters and then there's the slaves.**

And that isn't correct.

Don't expect these inconvenient facts to sway Obama in his quest for the presidency. And if he is elected, and Democrats also sweep both houses of Congress, we are going to see the most liberal crowd in Washington since the New Deal, convinced of their mandate to drive up taxes in fond hope of greatly expanding their socialist vision of American government.

# 14. Abortions For All, Guns For None?

If there are two issues—*life and death issues*—on which Obama is entirely out of step with the majority of the American people, it is the sanctity of life and guns.

**Obama would put a gun to the head of an unborn child but ban all other uses of that gun.** It's patently difficult to believe, but it is the situation.

Obama portrays himself as a thoughtful, progressive fellow who carefully considers all sides of a controversial issue before making a decision. Yet his actual voting record on abortion puts him further out in left field than even the militant abortionists at NARAL Pro-Choice America. Far from thoughtful, that's thoughtless.

As an Illinois lawmaker, Obama had a chance to vote on the "Induced Infant Liability Act" – legislation designed to address cases where, during an abortion procedure, the infant is actually born. The Act would have banned killing of that living child.

This is the easiest of bills for a legislator to support, no matter his or her political leanings, because it speaks to the baby that is out of the womb, alive. And still Obama voted it down. He would kill the baby.

While he was voting to "kill the baby" the U.S. Congress was considering a similar federal law, known as the Born Alive Infant Protection Act. Again it was an easy bill to pass; the Senate passed it unanimously on a voice vote; the House passed it overwhelmingly. Even Hillary Clinton, Ted Kennedy, and Barbara Boxer voted for it. These are among the most liberal, pro-abortion leaders in the Democratic Party. They concluded that protection of a child who survives an abortion was no threat to Roe vs. Wade. Not so, Obama. He believes an abortionist should have the right to kill a baby after the moment of birth.

Even the folks at NARAL Pro-Choice America took a very public position in favor of the child-protection legislation:

> Consistent with our position last year, NARAL does not oppose passage of the Born Alive Infants Protection Act… floor debate served to clarify the bill's intent and assure us that it is not targeted at Roe v. Wade or a woman's right to choose.[127]

Still, Obama voted against the Illinois version of the bill. That suggests that **his vote was not an effort to curry favor with the pro-abortionists but a genuine expression of his heart.**
*"Kill the baby."*
So genuine, that he voted consistently over time. The first time the Induced Infant Liability Act came up in the Judiciary Committee, he voted "present" which means "NO" because it stops the bill from leaving committee. The bill came up again, and this time Obama was clear as an infant's eyes: *"NO!"*

Sponsors of the bill then sent it to another Senate committee, in hopes of a better reception. They chose the Senate's Health and Human Services Committee. Bad choice. Obama chaired that committee and exercised his prerogative to bury the bill so that it, like so many babies, would never see the light of day.

There is no mistaking this track record, or the stark implications for abortion policy in an Obama presidency.

## Obama supports third-trimester abortions

In his gentle and breezy speeches to general audiences, Obama comes across as quite the reasonable and thoughtful guy. When speaking to activists, he throws big slabs of red meat. He is a politician—he panders to the prejudices of his audiences. This can make it difficult to gauge his true thinking. The most reliable gauge, then, is the litany of promises Obama has made to special interest groups. For he will be pressured to keep these promises. Speaking to abortion advocates in July 2007, Obama promised:

> *The first thing I'd do as President is sign the Freedom of Choice Act.*

**The Freedom of Choice Act would override every single state law limiting or regulating abortion.** It would also override the federal ban on partial birth abortion. As justification for his position, Obama opened a window into the deep legal thinking he brings to this issue:

> *I am absolutely convinced that culture wars are so nineties; their days are growing dark, it is time to turn the page... We want a new day here in America. We're tired about arguing about the same ole' stuff. And I am convinced we can win that argument.*[128]

This man taught constitutional law at the University of Chicago?

Shortly after the Supreme Court decided in 2007 to uphold the ban on *partial birth* abortions, Obama went before a national meeting of Planned Parenthood and condemned the high court's decision, calling it *"a concerted effort to steadily roll back"* legal abortions. Once again, this is not Roe v. Wade territory; these are partial birth abortions at issue. The child is alive, but Obama wants it dead.

Columnist Star Parker captured the flimsy pretense of Obama's legal condemnation, as well as the wrenching horrors that Obama would wish on this country:

> *Criticizing Justice Anthony Kennedy, who wrote the majority opinion in the case, Obama said, 'Justice Kennedy knows many things, but my understanding is that he does not know how to be a doctor.' Of course, Kennedy's job is not to be a doctor, but to be a judge. And in doing so, he included in his opinion testimony*

*of a nurse who participated in a partial birth abortion procedure:*

*'The baby's little fingers were clasping and unclasping, and his little feet were kicking. Then the doctor stuck the scissors in the back of his head, and the baby's arms jerked out ... The doctor opened up the scissors, stuck a high powered suction tube into the opening, and sucked the baby's brains out ... Now the baby went completely limp. He threw the baby in a pan, along with the placenta, and the instruments he had just used.'[129]*

In his speech to the folks at Planned Parenthood, Obama went on to differentiate McCain's pledge of "judicial constraint" from his own brand of "legal activism." Obama pledged to appoint judges *"who are sympathetic to those who are on the outside, those who are vulnerable, those who are powerless."*

If Obama and his audience of abortion activists are at all aware of the irony of his appointing judges who will protect the most powerless of all—the helpless infant, it was lost to the thundering applause that day.

On the 35th anniversary of Roe v. Wade, many Americans are clearly invested in keeping abortion legal. But few Americans with conscience believe in the killing of a baby beyond the moment of birth. Obama believes in it. He is the most radically left-wing member of the Senate on the sanctity of life.

Feeling thusly, it is no wonder that Obama also seeks to hand more and more parental duties over to the government, specifically to the United Nations.

Obama supports the UN Convention on the Rights of the Child and wants this UN treaty to be the supreme law of the land. He hasn't said as much. But he knows that if the law treaty is ratified, it will constitutionally override state laws. Columnist Michael Ferris explains the meaning of this:

*The Committee on the Rights of the Child is the official UN tribunal granted the authority to interpret and*

211

*enforce the Children's Convention, which sets forth an exhaustive index of children's rights, many at odds with the rights of parents. The tribunal has held, for instance, that the United Kingdom violated children's rights in Wales by allowing parents to withdraw their children from public school programs without first considering the child's wishes.*[130]

Obama would have the UN (the world's most dysfunctional organization with a Commission on Human Rights headlined by such family-first nations as Zimbabwe, Saudi Arabia and Syria) decide what is best for our children, intervene in decisions regarding our children's education, and choose whether the child's wishes or the parent's wishes are the best for the child. Maybe Obama believes in UN supervision because he saw almost zero parenting in his South Chicago district. But for the great majority of us Americans who are quite capable of raising children, thank you, but no thank you to more government.

## Planned Parenthood to become a federal agency?

With everything we've heard from Obama, it is not hard to imagine a President Obama proudly announcing the formation of a new cabinet level agency, *The Department of Planned Parenthood*. Such a move would lock-in ever increasing federal funding for his pet agency.

We have no independent confirmation that this is Obama's intention. But we would not be surprised. Though, Obama may find the agency name too restrictive for his tastes. He may prefer *The Department of Planned Life*.

As we write, the California Supreme Court has ruled that same-sex marriage is a "right." California joins Massachusetts in rewriting marriage laws. As other states with leftist legislatures join in, all of America will see the spectacle that's been going on in these two states: Mayors standing on the steps of City Hall, marrying two men or two women, and passerby families rushing their children off in another directions in hopes of not having to explain what their young children are seeing.

In April 2008 Obama granted an interview to *Advocate. com*—the lesbian, gay, bisexual, and transgender news site. Obama boasted that he's on top of the lesbian, gay, bisexual, and transgender cause:

> *I think that it is absolutely fair to ask me for leadership… I'm ahead of the curve on these issues compared to 99% of most elected officials around the country.*

Getting out ahead of the curve for Obama means repealing the Defense of Marriage Act. In his campaign literature targeted to this special interest group, Obama writes:

> *We need to fully repeal the Defense of Marriage Act.*

Repealing the act would force the other 48 states to "recognize" the same-sex marriages that have been made a right in Massachusetts and California. Of course Obama doesn't want his promise to the cross-dressers to cross over into the mainstream of America. So after meeting with them, he rushed to the nearest video camera to insist that he fully respects the right of states to determine their own marriage laws. His handlers issued this statement:

> *Obama has always believed that same-sex couples should enjoy equal rights under the law… he respects the decision of the California Supreme Court and continues to believe that states should make their own decisions when it comes to the issue of marriage.*[131]

So we have one Obama saying he will force states to allow same-sex marriages, and the other Obama saying the states can make their own decisions. One of these Obamas is lying.

This is the Obama pattern of political expedience—saying whatever an audience wants to hear, rather than what he believes.

It is a pattern that extends from the sanctity of life to the fundamental right to bear arms.

## Trying to doubletalk gun owners.

Pennsylvania boasts the highest per-capita membership in the NRA. When Obama campaigned there, his handlers fanned out among the crowds to make it clear that Obama is an ardent supporter of Second Amendment rights. It was desperation politics in action, since only days before Obama had told the groovy set in San Francisco that Pennsylvanians cling to their guns because they are bitter about their pitiful little lives.

Obama was facing a tough crowd.

Unsurprisingly, he lost that state's Democratic primary to Hillary. His comments about the endemic bitterness of the locals may have contributed to his loss. Or maybe it was Obama's 1999 attempt to pass a federal law prohibiting the operation of any gun store within five miles of a school or park. While on paper this sounds decent enough, Pennsylvanians surely knew that the law would eliminate gun stores from the entire inhabited portion of Pennsylvania and other states. **Gun stores would have to move out into the empty deserts.**

Or maybe Pennsylvanians heard about a questionnaire Obama filled out back in 1996, calling for a total ban on all handguns. His handlers claim that Obama *"never saw or approved the questionnaire"* and that an aide filled it out incorrectly. But the fact-checkers looked over the questionnaire and found Obama's own handwriting all over it. Busted.

Or maybe Pennsylvanians know of Obama's support for the overturned Washington, D.C. handgun ban—a ban that's similar to the one he helped pass for the Chicago suburbs. Obama's anti-gun bias was even more evident back in Chicago in 2004, when he voted against a bill to give legal protection to citizens who violate handgun bans when using those handguns in self-defense on their own property. The law passed, despite Obama's opposition. But his position was clear:

*If someone breaks into your home,*
*sorry—but you may not defend yourself.*

Once again, those who listen to Obama's public speeches or visit Obama's website will hear what sounds like a reasonable man. His website touts his belief in the Second Amendment rights to have guns *"for the purposes of hunting and target shooting."*

What he doesn't refer to is the right to have firearms to defend one's self, home and family. That is conspicuously absent. And that would make Obama, according to John Sigler of the NRA, *"the most antigun politician ever to set foot in Washington."*

An Obama presidency would give federal sanction to a long-held liberal conviction that "gun owners are no better than criminals." We would see federal muscle put behind Obama's long list of anti-gun legislation and policy positions:

- **Banning all handguns**
- **Banning the sale or transfer of all semiautomatic firearms**
- **Banning the Right-to-Carry in every state nationwide**
- **Banning firearms in the home, even for self-protection**

While Obama's contempt for our Second Amendment freedoms has spurred him to take action, his concerns about armed and violent criminals have been few, to the point of inaction.

In 1999 legislation that would have prosecuted teenage gang-bangers as adults when they fire a gun on or near school grounds, Obama voted *"Present"* -- the functional equivalent of *"NO"*!

In a 2001 vote to control gang violence by making gang-bangers eligible for the death penalty, Obama voted "NO"!

215

As if to crystallize his positions on violent crime, Obama told the *Chicago Tribune* that he believed federal sentencing laws used to put armed and violent predators behind bars should be abolished!

Then if those same violent criminals turn around and attack you, Obama opposes your right to protect yourself.

It is the government's job, Obama maintains instead, to protect you and care for you.

The Supreme Court wisely threw out the District of Columbia's 32-year-old anti-gun law, the most restrictive in the nation. In so doing, the Court finally defined the Framers' intent with respect to the 2nd Amendment: Citizens have a fundamental right to own a gun for the purpose of protecting home and family. And what was Obama's take on the ruling?

> *I have always believed that the Second Amendment protects the rights of individuals to bear arms ... but I also identify with the need for crime-ravaged communities to save their children from the violence that plagues our streets ...* [132]

A typical Obama wiffle-waffle. Makes your head spin.

# 15. A Neosocialist Government?

Thus far in our unmasking of Barack Hussein Obama, we've revealed two of the core values that animate the man and inform his political judgment. His handlers have certainly worked hard to mask over these values, as they are not shared by more than 25% of the electorate at most. But they remain the stuff of which Obama is made.

The first is an inherent *trust* that government can solve whatever problems the good citizens of this country may face. The second is a *distrust* of capitalism as an engine of economic betterment for all. These twin values complement each other, and form the underpinning of the neosocialist state view.

Interestingly, this idea of a new approach to a socialist paradise first gained popularity in 1930s Europe, particularly in France. Some have speculated that the neosocialist fervor of the time softened France for an easy invasion by German shock troops, but that invasion was likely to have succeeded anyway. French neosocialists were keen on tossing off the angry old Marxism and replacing it with a "constructive revolution" headed by government technocrats. In their view, an authoritarian state could be a benevolent state, replacing soulless capitalism with a planned economy built on the solidarity of the working class.

From this description, it may sound like we are disparaging neosocialists. Not at all. We are merely summarizing their own literature. This is their view of themselves, free of editorial.

Obama's political compass skews a little to the right of the classical neosocialists because time has marched on. In the 1930s there was a yearning among workers for fair wages, employee rights, and unionization. These yearnings became demands that were eventually met—at least in Europe and the United States. So the neosocialist agenda has evolved, as well. But its core utopian ideal remains essentially the same: *The desire for all people on the planet to live equally well.* This desire beats strongest today in the hearts of idealists, dreamers and, occasionally, a Presidential candidate.

As a political agenda, **this desire translates into "plums for the people" and "bulldogs for businessmen."** It's a hike down the road from a chicken in every pot. But it is the agenda Obama has laid out for his presidency, as we see in this chapter.

## Replacing free trade with fierce protectionism.

Democratic candidates for President have a long history of campaigning as "tough on trade" to lock in the union vote, but once in office, they govern as free traders. Knowing this, a lot of business leaders are expecting Obama to cast off his naïve protectionist rhetoric, face the reality of the world we live in, and push hard for free trade around the globe.

They may be sorely disappointed.

This election will be unlike the previous several.

Public opinion has shifted against free trade—not only as an ideal, but in practice. Congress is now populated by anti-free trade activists, and their numbers will increase after the 2008 elections. The unusually long primary season has given special interest groups an opportunity to secure promises from Obama on a detailed list of trade issues. It will be next to impossible for Obama to wiggle out of these promises, even if he wanted to do it. And there is no evidence that he wants to based on the speeches he has given and the books he has written:

> ... free trade may well grow the worldwide economic pie—but there's no law that says workers in the United States will continue to get a bigger and bigger slice. [133]

Obama is correct, as far as he takes the analysis. And he concludes that the workers of this country need government to ride to their rescue:

*...we can only compete if our government makes the investments that give us a fighting chance—and if we know that our families have some net beneath which they cannot fall. That's a bargain with the American people worth making.*[134]

To strike this bargain with the American people, Obama has gone on record as saying he will rewrite NAFTA—the North American Free Trade Agreement with Canada and Mexico. He may even sack the whole deal.

He will rip up any trade pacts that George Bush succeeds in getting through Congress.

He will designate China as a currency manipulator.

And he will delve into the minutia of hundreds of World Trade Organization agreements.

None of this makes for good sound bites on the evening news, so you won't hear much about it from Obama, McCain or anyone in the media interested in keeping their ratings high. But each of us will feel the effects of any wholesale changes in our nation's trade policies.

**And if the next President is not careful in the handling of global trade, we could see our nation's prosperity stumble and fall harder than at anytime since the spring of 1930.**

With the Great Depression lying over America like a wet wool blanket in 1930, and an entire nation clamoring for relief, Congress responded with the Smoot-Hawley Act. This bill jacked up U.S. tariffs on some 20,000 imported goods so high that other countries retaliated, jacking up their own tariffs. As a result, U.S. exports plunged by nearly half.

None of this happened in a vacuum. Congressmen were privately admitting at the time that it was the stupidest thing they had ever done. *The New York Times* headline of May 5th screamed, "1,028 Economists Ask Hoover to Veto Pending Tariff Bill." But like Congress, Hoover was spooked by the protectionist hysteria that was sweeping the country. No veto came. And in the end, Smoot-Hawley probably deepened the Great Depression, and contributed as well to the rise of Nazi Germany and the Japanese attack on Pearl Harbor.

Good people can argue over the *actual* long-term repercussions of Smoot-Hawley, but there is no disagreeing that the Act itself was a desperate response to a nation mired in the deepest economic misery since Jamestown 1607.

We are facing no such misery in America now. We are facing tough hurdles, but that is the way of things. Any Presidential candidate who seriously intends to start a "trade war" has to be an errand boy for a narrow special interest …

## Promising the world to the union bosses.

> ***Teamsters:*** *Senator, this great union has been under a consent decree for almost 20 years. It's been humiliated, scrutinized, raked for millions …*

> ***Obama:*** *If you've got somebody in the White House who you know, who you trust and who you have got a history with, then you're going to see a change in terms of how we evaluate these consent decrees …*

> Above is the kind of conversation that candidates have,

which seldom make the news. In this case, we capture Obama in the midst of selling his soul to the Teamsters Union. The Teamsters have long chafed under the weight of government consent decrees—a fancy term for "staying out of jail." The Teamsters claim they aren't as corrupt as they used to be, and so they shouldn't have the Feds watching their every move any more. Right or wrong, they were able to extract a promise from Obama to turn down the heat. In March 2008, the Obama campaign released a statement:

*It is time for the Justice Department to begin negotiations with the Teamsters regarding the elimination of the IRB and alternatives that will put the union's future back in the members' hands.*

So Obama is committed, and without wiggle room. This is only one of many promises he made to the union—promises he'll be hard-pressed to renege on.

**Nobody is grinning wider at Obama's candidacy than the union bosses. This election is their best shot in a half-century of making over Washington.** If they can capture the White House, the House of Representatives, and a filibuster-proof Senate, they are looking at the biggest rewrite of labor law in modern America. For the unions, Obama has been a long time in coming.

George W. Bush gave the unions eight years of corruption probes and forced more openness in their financial dealings. Bill Clinton gave them NAFTA. George H.W. Bush allowed workers to withhold the political dues they pay unions. Ronald Reagan famously broke the air traffic controllers union. During this time the U.S. workforce came to see little value in unions, and today only 7.4% of private sector workers are members of a union.

Union bosses are well aware that their days were numbered until Obama came along. And they are sparing no expense in getting him elected.[135]

- The AFL-CIO and its affiliates have raised an unprecedented $250 million to put 200,000 union workers to work campaigning for Obama in the crucial final weeks.

- The National Education Association has ponied up $50 million.

- The Service Employees International Union has added $100 million to actually pay 2,000 union members to leave their jobs and go work on Democratic campaigns.

221

All totaled, unions are expected to spend more than $1 billion of their members' money on the 2008 elections. And what are they expecting to receive in return?

- **Unions want** Obama to rewrite our country's trade agreements so as to favor union workers and jeopardize the ability of business to compete

- **Unions want** Obama to shelve longstanding rules that require unions to work with management when organizing employees

- **Unions want** Obama to repeal parts of the 1947 Taft-Hartley Act that have allowed 22 states to enact "right to work" laws and be more competitive

- **Unions want** Obama to set aside government projects that only unionized companies can bid on

- **Unions want** Obama to boost unemployment insurance benefits

- **Unions want** Obama to penalize companies that hire overseas

- **Unions want** Obama to require small companies of under 20 employees to allow union organizers in the doors

- **Unions want** Obama to rework job definitions to bring more positions under the union umbrella

And lastly, unions want the Department of Labor to take a siesta and turn a blind eye to union shenanigans even while beefing up regulatory oversight of business in general.

Obama will not speak much about his promises to unions in this campaign, unless forced. Republicans had better ask how our country can compete in a global economy when workers' demands force good companies into losing competitive positions.

# Destroying what's left of quality healthcare.

> *… I believe in universal healthcare…*
> *anybody who wants healthcare under*
> *my plan will be able to obtain it.*

We'd like to ask a question of Obama: "If your wife Michelle or your daughters Malia and Natasha were seriously injured, and they needed the best medical care available, would you try to obtain it for them?"

Being a bright guy, we don't imagine Obama would take the bait. He'd say instead that (1) his healthcare plan has nothing to do with wealthy folks like him—wealthy folks can always get great care; (2) his plan has everything to do with millions of uninsured and underinsured people; (3) America is a big, prosperous, compassionate nation and if there are people among us who cannot afford to pay for healthcare, then we owe it to ourselves to help them.

He is wrong on all three points.

Obama would turn every physician into an employee of the state, with their right to practice medicine proscribed by a bunch of bureaucrats who've never taken an anatomy course. When this happens, the willingness of doctors to practice medicine declines.

Orthopedic surgeons require four years of college, four years of medical school, five years of residency, and often another two years in a specialty fellowship and even a year of research. That's a lot of years, and it begins with medical school loans of $200,000 or so. How many people are going to put themselves through all of this—only to come into a system where your income is restricted, your every move is proscribed by some bureaucrat in Washington, and your patients increasingly come to despise you because you're the human face of a system that doesn't work?

**And if we lose our best and brightest, if we bleed away the vitality of a market-based healthcare system, where do the**

**wealthy folks go for the best care? France? England? If it's not going to be America, where's it going to be?**

What if Obama wins and anyone who wants healthcare can get it? How will ObamaCare be executed? What would be covered? Would everyone get free ambulance rides? Free aromatherapy treatments? Free nose jobs? Free breast implants? And who makes these decisions? Some sociology major fresh out of college in his first "real" job in Washington?

Then there's the cost of complying with all the government rules. There are over 100,000 pages of federal regulations now; doctors can't hope to understand them all, much less follow them! It's a very inefficient engine. Obama wants to give us more regulations?

Think about it. What is the major complaint that folks have with their doctor?

People feel they don't get enough time with their doctor or, worse yet, they don't even have access to their doctor. With the plans Obama has been outlining, it's going to get worse.

Given all the problems we can anticipate in universal healthcare, how does an intelligent man like Obama still argue for it?

Because the driving emotion behind the liberal desire for national healthcare is that everybody should have exactly the same healthcare. Obama is willing to reduce the *quality* of healthcare in order to ensure a greater *quantity* of healthcare. And he thinks government can make this happen.

In fact, more people *could* obtain good healthcare if not for people like Obama. When he was an Illinois Senator, Obama voted 18 times to *require* insurance to cover medical procedures. And which procedures?

Laughing gas in the dentist office. Infertility treatments. Drug rehab. Injuries from being drunk. **Obama says people lack health insurance because "they can't afford it." He's right. And he is also partly responsible.** The Council for Affordable Health Insurance figures that these "mandates" from the politicians drive up healthcare costs 20% to 50%, depending on the state.[136]

Another reason health insurance is so expensive: there's no real competition. The industry is heavily regulated by Washington and as a result the costs have skyrocketed. Competition would bring down costs. But under Obama, there will be more regulation, less competition. So costs will continue to rise.

Places like Yuma, Arizona, already offer a frontline view of medicine the way Obama likes it. For an average doctor in Yuma, 70% of patients are on Medicare, 25% are on a state-run medical program called Access, and 2% are on private insurance. Yuma is already operating under a very socialized medical environment.

The result is a deadly combination—a serious shortage of physicians, and long lines of people waiting to get treatment. Some have the sniffles, so they go to the hospital. Some have a broken arm, so they go to the hospital. But they all have one thing in common: they have made an economic decision about healthcare. They've determined that they can spend their money on other things – cars, motorcycles, toys – and not worry about buying any kind of health insurance because they know the government will take care of them. They know that when they come to the emergency room, they're going to get free care.

When medical care is given away, it is not valued. It's always easier to spend somebody else's money. That's human nature. And how much easier is it to spend someone else's money? The RAND Health Insurance Experiment conducted on 2,000 families between 1974 and 1982 found that people getting "free care" from government were 28% more likely to use medical services, 67% more likely to see a doctor, and 30% more likely to be admitted to the hospital than those paying for service. All in all, it costs 45% more to have socialized medicine.[137]

**Thus with healthcare spending in the U.S. now topping $2.3 trillion, ObamaCare would thus add ONE TRILLION DOLLARS to government spending. Or about $6,000 per taxpayer. But we can afford it, Obama says, revealing more about the depth of his concern than the depth of his solution.**

## Censoring conservatives on the radio.

If the aim is a transformation from a "capitalist opportunity society" to a "socialist equality society" the last thing you want to listen to on the radio is those pesky conservatives who are so darn happy with the status quo. So what do you do?

If you are Obama and you have a Democratic-controlled Congress backing you up, you restore the "Fairness Doctrine" that Ronald Reagan's FCC kiboshed. Until Reagan killed it, this federal rule required radio and TV stations to give equal time to both sides of any public policy discussion. This sounds like a fair enough policy, at first anyway.

In reality, restoring the Fairness Doctrine would end political talk as we know it. Glenn Beck, Sean Hannity, Mark Levin, Rush Limbaugh, Michael Medved, Melanie Morgan, Bill O'Reilly, Chris Plante, Michael Savage, Michael Reagan, Debbie Schlussel, Brian Sussman, Kirby Wilbur and other stalwarts of conservative thought would be muzzled. But why only conservatives?

That's what makes the Democrats' attack so offensive and mean-spirited. They will never have to say they are muzzling the radio talkers they so despise. To the contrary, they can publicly claim to be seeking fair debate on the nation's airwaves, an obligation they take very seriously since the airwaves are publicly owned.

Meanwhile in private, **Obama's regulatory police at the FCC will begin investigating every radio station** in America to ensure compliance with the new regulations. They'll be asking if a Michael Medved received more airtime on the last seven Tuesdays than Randi Rhodes of Air America did. That Medved has an audience with eager advertisers and Air America has some limousine liberal footing the bills, is of no matter to the airwave police. And radio station owners, fearing lawsuits and federal sanctions, will buckle under and cancel conservative programming.

Talk radio and independent news sources will be regulated to the point that they are effectively silenced.

## Strangling business with sweeping new regulations.

As you'll recall, Obama's first job out of Columbia University was with a company involved in international trade, and he loathed every aspect of it. To his biographer, he admitted to being off-put by the *"coldness of capitalism."* To his Communist Party mentor of the time, he said he felt like *"a spy behind enemy lines."* And lest there be no mistaking Obama's feelings about the greatest economic engine the world has ever known, Obama wrote passionately in his memoirs of the *"the real enemy"* being the *"investment bankers"* and *"fat-cat lobbyists."*

Obama lasted in that job barely a year—not even enough time to beat the learning curve. And based on that firsthand experience in the business world, Obama feels he is the man to overhaul the entire regulatory framework of the business world. He has called the regulation of business *"disjointed and ineffective,"* and in need of a centralized regime to oversee the risks of the marketplace. When the subprime-mortgage crisis hit, Obama had the platform he sought:

> When subprime-mortgage lending took a reckless and unsustainable turn, a patchwork of regulators were unable or unwilling to protect the American people.

Obama knows just what to do about that patchwork of regulators—assemble legions of government overseers to weave a more protective blanket for the American people. But what do those overseers bring to the task? As much business experience as Obama?

## Hey all you in the Middle East, "Get along!"

One of the deepest urges of the neosocialist is to be able to gather everyone around the campfire, lock arms and sing a ghazal (the Muslim version of Kumbaya). This behavior can be chalked up to an overdeveloped sense of moral relativism, yes. But often it is much less. Often it is a dreamy wistfulness, a poetic ideal inspired by Thoreau at his pond or, say, Jews and Arabs rejoicing in their shared humanity. It is, in short, *the art of the potential*. Sweet and endearing in our children and college professors, this utopian thinking is a clean miss on the obvious: politics is, in short, *the art of the possible*.

In politics, you don't get to do what you'd love with the situation you'd like, you do what you can with the situation you have. And so when Obama told supporters in Des Moines in March 2007 that *"nobody is suffering more than the Palestinian people,"* he appeared to be speaking not only his convictions, but his fondest desire that suffering be eliminated from this world.[138] But when convictions collide with desires, it can get messy. For in fact Obama went on in that speech to say the Palestinians were suffering as a result of *"the stalled peace efforts with Israel."*

No gaffe. Obama knew the score. He knew his views were offensive to American Jews, so be it. Then his handlers waterboarded some sense into him, apparently. Because a month later at the South Carolina Democratic debate Obama insisted that his remarks had been taken out of context (again) and in fact he had always meant to say:

> *Nobody has suffered more than the Palestinian people from the failure of the Palestinian leadership to recognize Israel, to renounce violence, and to get serious about negotiating peace and security for the region.*[139]

That's now his story, and he's sticking to it. Knowing that Jews historically vote Democratic, Obama kept on the offensive. He arranged an interview with the *Atlantic Monthly* to cement his 11th hour conversion to "friend of Israel":

> *The idea of a secure Jewish state is a fundamentally just idea, and a necessary idea, given not only world history but the active existence of anti-Semitism, the potential vulnerability that the Jewish people could still experience.*

Perhaps Obama's sudden conversion is sincere. Perhaps we should take him at his word. The worst thing that could happen to Israeli and American Jews would be for dark suspicions about Obama to become self-fulfilling prophecies.

Just because his name is Barack Hussein Obama.

Just because the Democratic Party has a long record of equivocation in the Middle East, with Jimmy Carter running around accusing Israel of outright *apartheid*. Call old Jimmy a nut, or maybe he's just speaking his true convictions, no longer standing on ceremony. Maybe he's saying what Obama's thinking. It's hard to know from the continued statement/retraction pattern of Obama's.

Take this example. Early in the campaign, Obama received an endorsement from a senior leader of the Hamas terrorist group. Embarrassed, sputtering, Obama blurted out that of course he would never negotiate with, much less accommodate Hamas. So it had to be embarrassing, and telling, when just two days later, Obama's senior advisor on the Middle East admitted that he had in fact held a number of meetings with Hamas and he had argued for giving international aid to the terror group. The adviser was Robert Malley, and he was quickly shown the door—especially when the Jewish press learned that Malley had been arguing for U.S. support of Hamas at a time when they were lobbing more than 200 rockets a week into Israel's civilian neighborhoods.

**Obama surely knew his senior advisor was trashing Israel. Obama must have at least tacitly agreed, because Malley remained on the payroll for years—right up to the minute the press learned of his anti-Israel policies.**

So what does Obama really believe?

In the days following the Malley spectacle, Obama was again pleading for probationary "friend of Israel" status and beating down rumors that he is not now, nor has he ever been, a practicing member of the Muslim faith. But then he "stepped in it big" in Detroit's Joe Louis Arena.

In prepping for this Detroit event, one of Obama's aides waded into the crowd and asked two young men if they'd like to appear on stage with Obama. They were "stoked" by the idea, and the aide began briefing them. Then one asked if he could bring two lady friends along, and pointed to two women dressed in traditional, Muslim head coverings. The aide said "no."

Okay, no big deal. Team Obama has the right to project the image they desire from up on that stage. But even before Obama took the stage, the snubbed Muslim women had called a press conference at which they unleashed a world of hurt, concluding with a firm demand for an apology.

These Muslim agitators were clearly Obama supporters, and yet they were demanding an apology from him! So what did Obama do? He personally telephoned both women, and apologized. The very next day, the women "publicly" accepted Obama's apology on the pages of the *Detroit Free Press*.[140] But what exactly was Obama apologizing for? And why would Muslims believe they are "entitled" to appear on stage with a Presidential candidate?

Most importantly, **if Obama is so effortlessly forced to bend over for Muslims, how could he stand up to those Muslims who wish not to embarrass us, but to wipe us out?**

## Delivering $10 a gallon gas to a pump near you.

When prices at the pump blasted through $4 a gallon Americans got mad—fuming mad and looking for someone to blame. Acting swiftly, Obama released a series of TV ads with him walking through a gas station declaring that he'll slap a tax on the "*excess profits*" of ExxonMobil which, he claimed, were a massive $40 billion.[141]

Obama was right. Those were the oil company's profits for the last reporting period. And what do those profits represent? Dividend checks for millions of Americans, retirement income for firemen, teachers and plumbers, hopefulness for the future of our nation. But Obama wants to turn ExxonMobil into the bogeyman, as if somehow they are responsible for outrageous energy prices.

He need only look in the mirror to find the real culprit.

But first he needs to go back and retake those economics classes he missed in college. How is a higher tax on energy going to lower gas prices? When you tax an item, adding to its cost, you either end up with less of that item, or you pay more for that item. We believe it has something to do with supply and demand. But Obama would repeal that particular law of economics.

A similar windfall profits scheme was tried by Jimmy Carter back in 1980.[142] When the dust had all settled, the tax reduced our domestic oil production by 50% and doubled our imports from OPEC. This analysis was conducted by the nonpartisan Congressional Research Service. So when Obama pledges to lessen our dependence on foreign oil, he should know that his whopping windfall profits scheme accomplishes the exact opposite— shoveling billions more into the pockets of corrupt Mideast oil producers.

If ever confronted with arguments such as these, Obama would probably fire back that he's not opposed to business profit "per se" (something lawyers say when they're about to twist the truth), but since ExxonMobil is making "extra" profit solely because of the oil price spike, they should give those "extra" profits back.

Are ExxonMobil's profits truly extraordinary? Thomson Financial did a study. They found that in 2007, companies in the oil industry enjoyed profits of 8.3% on investment, versus the average for the hundreds of other industries of 7.8%. Big windfall? Then there's the study done by the Cato Institute. They looked at the years 1970 to 2003 and found the oil industry *"less profitable than the rest of the U.S. economy."*

If Obama has his way, oil companies will be even less profitable. Which brings us back to the mirror and the real reason we'll have $10 gas by the end of an Obama presidency.

Since the 1970s, liberals like Obama have fought against domestic crude oil production, and as a result, U.S. output has been cut almost exactly in half. Whereas we imported less than 25% of our oil in the 1970s, we now import 70% of our oil. Our nation has an estimated twenty year supply of oil and natural gas right off the coastline, but we've been denied access. We have even more oil reserves in the remote Alaskan wilderness; we would only need to "step on" about 2% of the local tundra to produce enough oil to drive down the global price and allow us to control our energy future.

Since the 1970s, liberals like Obama have also clamped down on the approvals process for new nuclear power plants, and zero have been built. As Kevin McCullough wrote so wonderfully in Townhall.com:

> *When it comes to crippling, racist, and economically debilitating energy policy liberals have truly paralyzed America. And they seem proud of their efforts. In the left's refusal to allow us to seek new energy sources they are stunting a nation's economy, they are hurting the average family, and they are starving hungry children... They also express abject resentment towards anyone who dares to mention the obvious—that it is their policies that put us in this mess to begin with and disallows our escape from it.*

Obama's energy liberalism is on display no better than in Kansas—a state desperate for additional electricity. Lawmakers there voted to boost the output of a coal-fired power plant. But then Obama's ally, Governor Kathleen Sibelius (a woman short-listed to become his Vice President) stepped in and vetoed the bill. Since coal is burned to supply about half the electricity in America, what alternatives would Obama and his fellow liberals offer us?

Wind power? Solar power? Biomass? Geothermal? We can all applaud the developments in these alternative energy sources. And we can argue for greater government investment in and tax incentives for energy R&D. But at present these alternative sources only meet 2.5% of our energy needs. Even if we manage to double production in the next five years, or triple or even quadruple throughput, it's still not going to replace our dependency on fossil fuel in our lifetimes. So what for now?

Ten dollar gas? With Obama in the Oval, probably.

## Appointing shifty radicals and Clinton retreads.

Among Beltway insiders and Washington pols who only stop to breathe between news cycles, the guessing game is roaring ahead in full glory: If elected, will Obama populate the thousands of senior Administration posts with his long-time Chicago cronies, or with anyone who wasn't indicated from the Clinton reign?

We expect both.

**John Kerry** shepherded Obama onto the national stage by selecting him to deliver the keynote speech at the 2004 Democratic National Convention. And Kerry had the good sense to endorse Obama over Hillary, an endorsement that helped Obama bounce back from his loss to Hillary in New Hampshire. Kerry has made it known he'd like to end his career as Secretary of State. If selected, Kerry would play a key role in reaching out to nations of the world who yearn for new leadership in the U.S., leadership that knows how to spread that American wealth around liberally.

Kerry's team at State would probably include **Robert Malley**, Obama's Mideast adviser until his contempt for Israel slipped into the public eye. Malley would like to be the Deputy for Middle Eastern Affairs. And George Soros would like that, as well, so it's a done deal.

Obama has made it clear that he would clean house at the Department of Justice, beginning with the Civil Rights Division. His stated first priority: launch a full-scale investigation of whether the Bush Administration violated the civil rights of any terrorists held in U.S. custody. A number of Former Clinton officials are expected to return to Justice to finish the work they began in the 1990s—handcuffing our intelligence agencies so they are ill-equipped to stop the next 9/11.

Obama's radical pal **William Ayres** has no remorse over the bombings and murders in his hate-America campaign. We've learned that Ayres has a keen interest in education—he's an ardent supporter of "Queering Elementary Education." He believes there's not enough gay sex ed in our grammar schools. Is he then a candidate for Secretary of Education?

While we're rummaging through Obama's Chicago attic, what about the **Reverend Jeremiah Wright**? Did he lose a shot at a government post by taking his loon-show public? Or was it all an act to allow Obama an easy denunciation of the man without upsetting black voters? We'll see if Wright takes over a new cabinet level agency in charge of paying massive reparations to the families of slaves.

The biggest guessing game in Washington is what Obama had to promise **Hillary** to keep her from plunging the knife she surely brought to their reconciliation meeting. And what, too, did Obama have to promise Bill Clinton—they are a two-fer, after all. Inside betting is that Hillary will get a seat on the Supreme Court and Bill will, at Hillary's secret directive, get the shaft. She's been waiting a long time for that.

Even the mere mention of Hillary on the Supreme Court should generate a rolling outrage across the country. How many times does one have to lie under oath or obstruct justice before being disqualified for the high court?

This is all speculation, of course. Maybe a President Obama would surprise us by appointing qualified blacks to senior posts. That would require him to reach across the aisle, of course. But he says he wants that.

# 16. Or Will We Unmask Obama in Time?

Few books are written in hopes of being dispensable in just a couple months—this is one of those books. Our earnest desire is to see this book remaindered on November 5, 2008, because a man named Barack Hussein Obama has been told by voters that he's not ready for such an important job.

But we also recognize that he has, statistically speaking, a 50/50 shot of becoming our 44th President. So we've looked ahead and tried to draw some conclusions about what America would look like after four years of Obama. Tagging it an Obamanation is good fun, with the added virtue of being technically correct. Tagging it with all proper seriousness is no easy task, however, and we apologize in advance for all the blunders we're sure to make.

**As the first U.S. President of African and Muslim heritage, Obama will be tested in ways never before seen.**

Deadly terrorists from the caves of Afghanistan to the camps of Iran may conclude that they can act with impunity—seizing oil assets, spreading *sharia* law to more nations, deposing weak governments, slaughtering innocent civilians, completing construction of long-range strategic nuclear weapons. **They've sized up Obama, and believe him incapable of striking a Muslim**. That makes him weak in their eyes. And weakness must be exploited.

Liberals will express genuine befuddlement that a man as peaceful and unassuming as Obama – *"he's not Bush, after all!"* – can incite such evil in the hearts of so many distant oppressors.

Having run on a platform of yanking the troops out of Iraq, he will find it very difficult to do. Just as Nixon ran on a pledge to get the U.S. out of Vietnam but took four long years to accomplish the task—and then only wretchedly, Obama will **take a full term**

**to exit Iraq**. And his friends at MoveOn.org will be less enthusiastic in endorsing four more years.

Eager to distract his partisans from the war in Iraq, which is now raging ahead on his watch, Obama will launch a big fiery populist crusade against corporate greed, golden-parachuting CEOs, tax-avoiding hedge-fund managers, and usurious credit card interest rates. A long line of recently fleeced consumers will be paraded before Congress to convince a nation that **tough new regulations are required to make capitalism more fair and equitable for all.**

Business leaders who had bought into the Obama rhetoric, and thought him a man of moderation, will be shocked by his Department of Labor's **stridency in prosecuting "abusive employers."** Smaller businesses will buckle under new federal regulations requiring them to open their doors to union organizers. An aggressive Equal Employment Opportunity Commission will **identify all manner of discrimination in the workplace**—such as hiring someone based on merit—and subpoenas will usher forth.

Keeping his pledge to raise taxes on just the top 20% of all income earners, Obama will get a firsthand lesson in economics as these top-earners seek clever and inventive ways to shelter income from taxation. As has happened every time taxes have been raised in the last 90 years, tax receipts will decline—Obama will have less revenue than he needs for his pet spending projects.

This time eager to distract folks from his domestic fiscal woes, Obama will convene a major summit of the world's leaders, leaking to the press that he had tidings of ominous import. That's when his Chief Science Advisor will announce that the globe is warming at an even more frightening clip than originally projected (totally confounding the scientists who had originally been paid to lie about climate statistics). In a frenzy to act before *"we're a goners,"* Obama will **create the "Office of Climate Control"** and locate it adjacent to the White House Correspondence Office, so that when the Oregon tree-huggers write long letters on recycled bark to express their fright over the end of life as we know it,

Obama's first responders will be able to send long thoughtful letters in reply.

ObamaCare won't come right away. After all, it can take months and months to figure out how to overhaul a two trillion dollar segment of the economy. But our nation's inexorable march toward universal care, already more entrenched in many areas than people realize, will continue onward. Then the most surprising thing will happen.

Obama will go on nationwide TV to proclaim that **while his healthcare plan has been an enormous success, and everyone who needs medical care can now get it, the costs have actually spiraled higher than originally anticipated**. Much higher. Especially when factoring in the cost of federally subsidized health insurance for 30 million illegal immigrants. And so while it is not his desire, he must again raise tax rates across the board.

Having already raised income taxes as promised, Obama will take heavy criticism for now having to **raise the top rate to over 40%,** and the national temper will flare when another twenty million people who thought of themselves as middle-class folks now find they're paying taxes in the top bracket. When they add up their tax bite from all levels of government, and find it topping 65% of their income—it will prompt two reactions:

1. **A national cry for a return to proven free market policies.**

2. **The first of many loud calls for Obama's impeachment.**

Obama will survive the clamoring voices of impeachment. Americans have grown tired of seeing our every President stalked and hounded to death—no matter the offense. This is less a reflection of Obama's resilience than the country's, and that is something to be celebrated.

There will be no celebrating in the nation's police stations, however. All kinds of new laws and mandates will show up on their desks, making life miserable, and more dangerous. Obama's proposal to lighten up the sentences for crack cocaine, for example, will **put dealers back on the streets almost immediately—** with fewer legal hurdles between them and our children.

As a creature of the neosocialist policies and Hollywood handlers who got him elected, Obama will be thrust into a number of embarrassing situations. His oldest daughter Malia will be of dating age, and will want to go to the latest Hollywood movie portraying the U.S. government as the source of evil, glorifying guilt-free adolescent sex, and urging freedom from responsibility for one's actions. Obama, in the role of father and head of state, will have to answer to Americans who wonder what kind of world he is leaving to his daughters.

## In Conclusion

In the case of Barrack Obama, what you see at first glance is not what you will get. He is a man with charisma, but he speaks vaguely about inspiring topics such as hope and change, avoiding substance.

Like the film starring Robert Redford, *"The Candidate,"* Hollywood and his handlers have taken the malleable and moldable candidate of Obama, a hunk of clay and created their perfect candidate.

By removing Obama's mask and examining the real man beneath, we see a much different person than he presents to mainstream America. His true beliefs and philosophies are extreme and dangerous in numerous ways.

Many people and philosophies have gone into shaping Obama into Hollywood's ideal candidate. Starting with his parents—both involved in Communist activities and subversive ideas, they had an impact on him. Both directly and indirectly. During his search and dreaming about the Muslim, African father who abandoned him, Obama made Barack Sr. into an ideal.

As a child in Jakarta, the Indonesian school and his step-father added another layer. Attending Columbia University, he developed a disdain for capitalism,

And to whom is Obama beholden?  What are the philosophies, ideals and beliefs he holds dear. We've tried to answer all of these questions in this book.

We may not have painted a perfect picture, but we hope this has given you a more complete insight into the real man behind the manufactured mask. We hope that this simple book has done what the Leftstream Media has refused to do. It has asked and tried to answer these questions.

We hope after reading this book, you will be in a better position to make an informed decision in November about the future direction of America. And win or lose we hope that you will join us in the daily battle to make America the greatest country in the history of civilization.

# NOTES

1. As reported by MSNBC, 5/7/08.

2. Nedra Pickler, Associated Press, 1/24/07.

3. Various secondhand sources including www. monstersandcritics.*com/news/usa/features/article_1411251.php*

4. Paul Watson, *Los Angeles Times*, reprinted in *Baltimore Sun*, *3/16/07.*

5. Aaron Klein, Obama anti-smear site: 'He was never a Muslim',
   *WorldNetDaily,* 6/12/08.

6. Aaron Klein, Obama anti-smear site: 'He was never a Muslim',
   *WorldNetDaily,* 6/12/08.

7. Jody Kantor, *The New York Times, 4/30/07.*

8. Barack Obama, *Dreams from My Father,* Three Rivers Press, 1995.

9. Nicholas D. Kristof, *The New York Times*, 3/6/07.

10. JPOST.COM STAFF, 6/12/08; photo of Barack and Malik from Israeli Insider: http://web.israelinsider.com/Articles/ Politics/12918.htm

11. http://www.barackobama.com/factcheck/2007/11/12/ obama_has_never_been_a_muslim_1.php

12. http://www.usvetdsp.com/jan08/obama_lou%20tribe.htm

13. http://kennethelamb.blogspot.com/2008/02/barak-obama-questions-about-ethnic.html

14. www.snopes.com/politics/obama/muslim.asp

15. Paul Watson, *Los Angeles Times*, March 16, 2007.

16. Andy Martin, Out2.com, 8/10/07.

17 Daniel Pipes, Obama and Islam, *FrontPageMagazine.com*, 12/24/07, 12/26/07.
18. James Taranto, Best of the Web, *Wall Street Journal,* 5/16/08.

19. David Mendell, *OBAMA: From Promise to Power*, page 44; HarperCollins , 2007.

20. Hank De Zutter, Lawyer, teacher, philanthropist, and author, *Chicago Reader*, 12/8/95.

21. David Mendell, *OBAMA: From Promise to Power*, page 62.

22. Barack Obama, *Dreams from My Father.*

23. Barack Obama, *Dreams from My Father.*

24. Barack Obama, *The Audacity of Hope, Crown 2006.*

25. Essay in *Chicago Tribune Magazine*, quoted from *OBAMA: From Promise to Power*, page 86.

26. David Mendell, *OBAMA: From Promise to Power*, page 87.

27. David Mendell, *OBAMA: From Promise to Power*, page 90.

28. infoplease.com/spot/bhmfirsts.html

29. David Mendell, *OBAMA: From Promise to Power*, page 15.

30. Shelby Steele, *A Bound Man*, Free Press, page 51.

31. Michelle Robinson's Princeton thesis excerpts obtained from various sources including http://www.politico.com/news/stories/0208/8642.html

32. Michael Reagan, The Other Obama, Townhall.com, 5/9/08.

33. David Mendell, *OBAMA: From Promise to Power*, page 104.

34. blogs.abcnews.com/politicalpunch/2008/02/michelle-obam-1.html

35. hotair.com/archives/2008/03/17/fournier-on-obama-its-the-arrogance

36. newsmax.com/fontova/obama cheguevara/2008/03/04/77631.html

37. freerepublic.com/focus/f-news/2017913/posts.

38. Michelle Malkin, Barack's Bitter Half, 5/7/08.

39. Originally at *Townhall.com* and referenced in a blog at http://www.politico.com/news/stories/0508/10472.html

40. Various news sources, including: Kathleen Parker, Oh Yes, He Will Make Us Better, *Townhall.com*, 5/21/08.

41. Conversation with David Mendell as reported in *OBAMA: From Promise to Power*, page 98.

42. Barack Obama, *Dreams from My Father*, 1995.

43. For more clarifying info, see *AmericanThinker.com*, June 2, 2008.

44. David Mendell, *OBAMA: From Promise to Power*, page 112.

45. Amanda B. Carpenter, Barack Obama Is Just Another Liberal, *HumanEvents.com*, 12/11/06.

46. Obama voted against SB 777 to end the unemployment insurance fund building tax; against SB 879 to end the minimum contribution tax rate for the unemployment system; against SB 795 to reduce employers' minimum contribution insurance rate.

47. David Mendell, *OBAMA: From Promise to Power*, page 125.

48. Barack Obama, *The Audacity of Hope*, page 18.

49. Wonkette Anna Marie Cox, 12/15/06.

50. According to the Congressional Quarterly.

51. Michelle Malkin, May 21, 2008.

52. John Fund, The Obama Gaffe Machine, *Wall Street Journal*, 5/30/08.

53. Brian Fitzpatrick, Media Cover Up Obama's Malaise Speech, *Townhall.com,* 5/20/08.

54. John Fund, Obama's Flaws Multiply, *Wall Street Journal*, April 15, 2008.

55. Robert B. Bluey, Unlike Kerry, Barack Obama Covets George Soros' Support, *CNSNews.com* Staff Writer, 7/27/04.

56. George Soros, in *The New York Review of Books*, 4/12/07.

57. freedomsenemies.com/_Obama/obamatimeline.htm

58. Jamie Glazov, The Shadow Party, *FrontPageMagazine.com*, 8/29/06.

59. Various news sources including: Rich Lowry, The Obama Rules, *National Review*, 5/12/08; Brent Bozell III, The Big, Bad, Right-Wing Wolf, 5/14/08.

60. Dorothy Rabinowitz, Obama's Media Army, *Wall Street Journal*, 4/23/08.

61. Jeff Johnson, *OneNewsNow*, 5/22/2008.

62. Bernard Goldberg, *Crazies to the Left of Me, Wimps to the Right*, Harper, 2007; page 188.

63. barackobama.com/2007/08/01/the_war_we_need_to_win. php

64. Chris Matthews Show, 10/21/06.

65. Quotes from various news sources including: http://www. usatoday.com/news/politics/election2008/2008-04-28-wright-press-club_N.htm; http://bumpshack.com/2008/03/18/pastor-jeremiah-wright-controversy-quotes

66. worldnetdaily.com/index.php?fa=PAGE.view&pageId=62911

67. Heather Robinson, Barack Obama: In Search of a Savior?, PoliticalMavens.com, 5/7/08.

68. Charles Krauthammer, Obama's Changing Moral Equivalence, *Wall Street Journal*, 5/2/08.

69 Various sources including: http://frontpagemag.com/Articles/Read.aspx?GUID=EA02DE98-ECD2-4DDF-AF24-E11003310D0C

70. tucc.org/talking_points.htm

71. Heather Mac Donald, Poisonous "Authenticity", *City-Journal*, 4/29/08.

72. Heather Mac Donald, The Wright Side of the Brain, *Wall Street Journal*, 4/30/08.

73. Shelby Steele, *A Bound Man*, page 54.

74. Star Parker, Is Obama really the man blacks need?, *Townhall.com*, 5/12/08.

75. Michael Reagan, The Other Obama, *Townhall.com*, 5/9/08.

76. Barack Obama, *The Audacity of Hope.*

77. http://www.billoreilly.com/column;jsessionid=FA68BDF155A C4B5466FF755B0E3B05AA?pid=23412

78. http://www.suntimes.com/news/mitchell/923055,CST-NWS-mitch30.article

79. http://www.youtube.com/watch?v=tIlIpOkRh2A

80. Cliff Kincaid, *Accuracy in Media*, 2/14/08.

81. Aaron Klein, Obama worked with terrorist, *WorldNetDaily. com*, 2/24/08.

82. Debbie Schlussel, Edward Said & "Inflexible Jews" Causing Mid-East Conflict: An Obama Insider Reveals the Real Barack, 1/30/08.

83. electronicintifada.net/v2/article6619.shtml

84. Nick Timiraos, Audience Member Quizzes Obama on Farrakhan, *Wall Street Journal*, 4/9/08.

85. Debbie Schlussel, Edward Said & "Inflexible Jews" Causing Mid-East Conflict: An Obama Insider Reveals the Real Barack, 1/30/08.

86. Various secondhand sources including: http:// bucknakedpolitics.typepad.com/buck_naked_politics/2008/04/ why-is-obama-hi.html

87. Mary Grabar, You Need a Weatherman To Tell Which Way Obama Will Go. *Townhall.com*, 6/22/08.

88. Various news sources including Ronald Kessler, Obama Embraces New Caustic Pastor, *Newsmax*, 5/8/08.

89. Source material includes Jacob Laksin, Obama's Newest Pastor Problem, *FrontPageMagazine.com*, 6/2/08.

90. Shaaban Abdel Rahim interview with Dar Al-Hayat as reported by James Taranto, Watch the Liberals Evade the Obvious, *Wall Street Journal*, 3/27/08.

91. Steve Chapman, Barack Obama and the Pertinent Precedents, *Townhall.com*, 1/17/07.

92. Tony Blankley, Race and the 2008 Election, *Townhall.com*, 5/14/08.

93. Bernard Goldberg, *Crazies to the Left of Me, Wimps to the Right*, Harper, 2007; page 36.

94. Shelby Steele, The Obama Bargain, *Wall Street Journal,* 3/18/08.

95. Shelby Steele, *A Bound Man*, page 61.

96. Shelby Steele, *A Bound Man*, page 70.

97. By Lara Setrakian, Obama: Investigate Duke Lacrosse DA Nifong, ABC News Law & Justice Unit, 3/25/07.

98. http://www.wikio.com/discussion/632070

99. Blogger at http://www.theblackrepublican.net/archives/004040.html

100. Ezra Klein, Obama's Gift, *The American Prospect*, 1/3/08.

101. Juan Williams, Obama and King, *Wall Street Journal*, 4/4/08.

102. http://www.barackobama.com/2007/03/04/selma_voting_rights_march_comm.php

103. http://hamptonroads.com/node/241601

104. TV ad on display at: http://www.rightpundits.com/?p=1195

105. http://classwarnotes.blogspot.com/2007/09/sen-barack-obamas-message-on-911.html

106. Remarks by Barack Obama, North Carolina primary victory speech.

107. Remarks to Cuban American National Foundation, 5/22/08.

108. Barack Obama interview with ABC News' Jake Tapper, 5/20/08.

109. John Bolton, Bring On the Foreign Policy Debate, *Wall Street Journal,* 5/19/08.

110. Conversation with David Mendell as reported in *OBAMA: From Promise to Power*, page 98.

111. Karl Rove, Obama's Troubling Instincts, *Wall Street Journal*, 5/22/08.

112. Bernard Goldberg, *Crazies to the Left of Me, Wimps to the Right*; page 170.

113. Philip Elliott, Obama Gets Warning From Friendly Voter, *The Associated Press*, 8/14/07.

114. Thomas Sowell, An Old Newness, *Townhall.com*, 4/29/08.

115. Thane Rosenbaum, Opinion Page, *Wall Street Journal*, 5/30/08.

116. ncpa.org/sub/dpd/index.php?Article_ID=16418

117. Democratic Presidential Debate; Howard University, 6/28/07.

118. OntheIssues.org, Democratic presidential debate, Los Angeles, 1/30/08.

119. whitehouse.gov/news/releases/2008/01/20080104-2.html

120. John F. Cogan and R. Glenn Hubbard, The Coming Tax Bomb, *Wall Street Journal*, 4/8/08.

121. See http://right-thinking.com/index.php/weblog/comments/stop_us_before_we_tax_again/

122. EDITORIAL STAFF, Obama's Tax Evasion, *Wall Street Journal*, 4/18/08.

123. EDITORIAL STAFF, Obama's Capital Loss, *Wall Street Journal*, 4/5/08.

124. Fund's Political Diary, Where Does Obama Invest His Money?, *Wall Street Journal*, 3/27/08.

125. Barack Obama, *The Audacity of Hope*, page 193.

126. Brad Schiller, The Inequality Myth, *Wall Street Journal*, 3/10/08.

127. Source material includes Amanda Carpenter, Obama More Pro-Choice Than NARAL, *HumanEvents.com*, 12/26/2006.

128. Peter Smith, *LifeSite News*, 6/10/08.

129. Source material includes Star Parker, Is Obama really the man blacks need?, *Townhall.com*, 5/12/08.

130. Source material includes Michael Farris, Obama Knows Best, *Townhall.com*, 5/14/08.